071324

Lazarus at the Table

Lazarus at the Table

Catholics and Social Justice

Bernard F. Evans

A Michael Glazier Book

LITURGICAL PRESS

Collegeville, Minnesota

www.litpress.org

A Michael Glazier Book published by Liturgical Press.

Cover design by David Manahan, O.S.B.
Photo by Andres Balcazar, iStockphoto.com.

2   3   4   5   6   7   8   9

Library of Congress Cataloging-in-Publication Data

Evans, Bernard F., 1943–
    Lazarus at the table : Catholics and social justice / Bernard F. Evans.
        p. cm.
    "A Michael Glazier book."
    Includes bibliographical references and index.
    ISBN-13: 978-0-8146-5114-8 (alk. paper)
    ISBN-10: 0-8146-5114-3 (alk. paper)
        1. Christian sociology—Catholic Church.   2. Christian sociology—United States.   3. Catholic Church—United States—Doctrines.   4. Church and social problems—United States.   5. Church and social problems—Catholic Church.   6. Christian ethics—Catholic authors.   I. Title.

BX1406.3.E94   2006
261.8088'282—dc22
                                                                2006009311

To Nancy,

*whose questions about Catholic social teaching
prompted the writing of this book*

Contents

Introduction

In the Gospel of Luke there is a story about a rich man and Lazarus (16:19-31). The wealthy man lived in comfort and feasted every day, while the poor Lazarus—sick and hungry—lay at the rich man's door hoping for crumbs that fell from his table. After death the rich man looked up from his torments in Hades to see Lazarus at the side of Abraham. He begged Abraham to send Lazarus to warn his brothers how they should live "lest they end up in this place of torment." Abraham replied: "They have Moses and the prophets. Let them listen to them . . . If they do not listen to Moses and the prophets, neither will they be persuaded if someone should rise from the dead" (16:27-31).

Our world is filled with opportunities to respond to Lazarus—to invite Lazarus to the table. We too have Moses and the prophets reminding us what it means to be in right relationship with God: to do justice, love tenderly, and walk humbly with God. We also have the words of Jesus from the last judgment scene in Matthew's gospel: "Whatever you did for one of these least brothers [and sisters] of mine, you did for me" (Matt 25:40).

In the Catholic Church we have a special set of writings designed to help us live the teachings of Jesus Christ in our contemporary world. Catholic social teachings show us how to contribute to the building of a more loving and just human community—a world "where freedom is not an empty word and where the poor man Lazarus can sit down at the same table with the rich man" (On the Development of Peoples, 47).

In their 2002 pastoral reflection, "A Place at the Table," the United States Catholic bishops remind us that we are a eucharistic people. When we gather around a table to celebrate, we should remember that this eucharistic event commits us to the poor. It commits us to making a place for Lazarus at the table.

Chapter 1

Catholic Social Teaching

What is Catholic social teaching? Why do we have it? Where does it come from? In recent years the Catholic bishops of the United States have written pastoral statements (e.g., on agriculture, on politics) and grounded them in the social teachings of the church. In the mid-1990s the bishops called on all Catholic education—parish catechesis, faith formation, schools, and seminaries—to make sure they are introducing all students and learners to these teachings. In their document, "Sharing Catholic Social Teaching," the bishops remind us that any Catholic education that does not include these teachings is not fully Catholic. So what are these teachings that we are called to incorporate into every form of Catholic education and faith formation?

Catholic social teaching is a body of doctrine developed by the church to help us apply the teachings of Jesus Christ to our communal, social life. It is an evolving set of moral teachings that addresses contemporary questions and issues in the social, economic, and political life of society and of the broader human community. These teachings can be rather demanding and unsettling to a comfortable, "settled in" churchgoer. It is in Catholic social teaching where we read that working for justice is a "constitutive dimension of the preaching of the Gospel," and that "no one may keep for himself what he does not need when others lack necessities," and that respect for life and for the dignity of the human person "extends also to the rest of creation which is called to join us in praising God."

These "modern Catholic social teachings," as they are sometimes called, have a long historical basis. They began to appear in a systematic

1

written form in the late nineteenth century, but their historical origins are rooted in Christian history. From the immediate post-biblical times to the present, the church has struggled to evaluate contemporary issues in the light of the gospel and the church's own teaching tradition. These teachings are a part of that effort.

Biblical Foundation

The primary foundation for Catholic social teachings is the Bible. The Scriptures provide the rationale for why the church and Christians need to be active in building a more just world. The biblical writings also indicate particular directions and emphases that our work for justice should reflect.

Central to this foundation for the church's social teachings is the biblical understanding of justice. In the Hebrew (Old Testament) scriptures, justice is presented as faithfulness to the expectations of a relationship. These biblical texts are concerned especially about the covenantal relationship between the people of Israel and their God. This relationship is forever shaped by God's delivering the people from slavery in Egypt— the story of the exodus. Their relationship with God reflects both the gratitude for what God has done for them already and the hope for what he will do in the days ahead.

This covenantal relationship carries some expectations of what the people are to do. As their God is unalterably faithful, so they too must be faithful to the demands of this relationship they have with God, this covenantal relationship. Two expectations are particularly central to the covenant between the Hebrew people and their God. One is that they shall worship no other God; Yahweh and he alone is their God, their only salvation. The second is that they shall love and care for one another, especially the poor and the marginalized among them. Their fidelity to the covenant and the demands of this relationship is modeled after the justice of God. The liberating event of the exodus from Egypt forms their experience of God. Theirs is a liberating, saving, and always faithful God. This is a God with a particular concern for the poor and the marginalized, such as they were while captives in Egypt. Fidelity to the demands of the covenantal relationship must include their own practical concern for the poor.

From time to time God sent prophets to tell the people of Israel that they were not living according to the expectations of their relationship with God. It was the task of the prophets to warn the people that they were not faithful to their covenantal relationship with Yahweh. What was the evidence of the people's unfaithfulness? It may have been false worship, or not trusting God and entering into alliances with other nations. So often the evidence of unfaithfulness was the people's refusal to care for the weak and the poor among them—the widows, the orphans, and the strangers.

Jeremiah lays out the conditions for the Hebrew people's return to right relationship with God.

> For if you truly amend your ways and your doings, if you truly act justly one with another, if you do not oppress the alien, the orphan, and the widow, or shed innocent blood in this place, and if you do not go after other gods to your own hurt, then I will dwell with you in this place, in the land that I gave of old to your ancestors forever and ever. (Jer 7:5-7)

The stranger, the orphan, and the widow were recognized as among the most vulnerable people in Jeremiah's society and culture. Treating well the marginalized and the powerless became a criterion as to whether justice was practiced.

When the people complained that God did not see their fasting, the prophet Isaiah reminded them that fasting which does not lead to care for the needy is useless.

> Is not this the fast that I choose: to loose the bonds of injustice, to undo the thongs of the yoke, to let the oppressed go free, and to break every yoke? Is it not to share your bread with the hungry, and bring the homeless poor into your house; when you see the naked, to cover them, and not to hide yourself from your own kin? Then your light shall break forth like the dawn, and your healing shall spring up quickly; your vindicator shall go before you, the glory of the Lord shall be your rear guard. Then you shall call, and the Lord will answer; you shall cry for help, and he will say, Here I am. (Isa 58:6-9)

Even the rest of God's creation is affected by the people's unfaithfulness to the expectations of their covenantal relationship with God. The prophet Hosea paints the mournful picture.

> There is no faithfulness or loyalty, and no knowledge of God in the land. Swearing, lying, and murder, and stealing and adultery break

out; bloodshed follows bloodshed. Therefore the land mourns, and all who live in it languish; together with the wild animals and the birds of the air, even the fish of the sea are perishing. (Hos 4:1-3)

The Hebrew scriptures also present rich images of life lived in faithfulness to God. The second chapter of Isaiah speaks of beating swords into ploughshares, of an end to all wars. This peaceful scenario comes only after the nations of the world decide to "go up to the mountain of the Lord, to the house of the God of Jacob; that he may teach us his ways and that we may walk in his paths" (Isa 2:3). Again in chapter eleven Isaiah presents the peaceable kingdom where the wolf and the lamb live together as do the calf and the lion. This kingdom of peace will come after "the earth will be full of the knowledge of the Lord" (Isa 11:9). Psalm 85 tells us that love and faithfulness will meet, that justice and peace will kiss, that "faithfulness will spring up from the ground and righteousness will look down from the sky" (Ps 85:10-12). Then even the land will increase its yield. The consequences of being in just relationships are peace, prosperity, and fertility on the land.

The biblical writings make it clear that Christians need to be engaged in the struggle to build a more just society. These writings also indicate where our efforts should fall. The prophets spoke about caring for the widows, orphans, and strangers. In the New Testament Jesus calls us to help the poor and the marginalized. At the start of his public ministry Jesus identified as his own the work of bringing good news to the poor, proclaiming release to captives, restoring sight to the blind, and granting freedom for the oppressed (Luke 4:18). In the parable of the last judgment, Jesus warns that we will be judged by how well we respond to the needs of the poor—with food, water, hospitality, visits to the sick and imprisoned. As long as you did it for one of these the least of my sisters and brothers you did it for me (Matt 25:31-46). The particular emphasis upon the poor that we find in Catholic social teaching has deep roots in the Bible.

Early Christian Writers

From the earliest days of the church, Christians have asked what it means to be a follower of Jesus Christ in contemporary society. How do we live our lives in faithfulness to our relationship with Christ? What do the gospels tell us about social issues of our day? During the first few centuries after Christ, the church struggled with these questions. Early

Christian writers and church leaders addressed topics and questions about Christians living in their society. Their issues were not all the same as the ones we face today. Remarkably, some of them were, and the way they addressed these issues has influenced Catholic social teaching in our time.

Early Christian writers had much to say about poverty, wealth, and the Christian's responsibility to those who are poor. We read in the Acts of the Apostles that the earliest Christian communities shared everything in common so that no one was in need. By the beginning of the third century some communities included persons of wealth. Clement of Alexandria felt the need to address the question of whether being wealthy was compatible with being a Christian. In his essay, "Christ the Educator," Clement noted that the desire for wealth is the source of trouble. One who possesses wealth should develop a spirit of detachment and be willing to lose it. Yet in another essay, "How Can the Rich Person be Saved?" Clement noted that it is possible to be wealthy and poor in spirit (16). Speaking to the more educated and more affluent, Clement of Alexandria encouraged Christians to share what they did not need and not try to distinguish too carefully between the deserving and the undeserving.

The clearest moral guideline for thinking about questions related to wealth, poverty, and our response to the poor was articulated in the fourth century by Ambrose of Milan. In *De Nabaoth* Ambrose argued that every person has a right to a share of God's gifts. He warned the greedy that their almsgiving is nothing more than restitution for stolen goods. "You are not making a gift of your possessions to the poor. You are handing over to him what is his" (*Nabaoth* 53). This principle of the universal destination of the goods of creation was held up as well by John Chrysostom, also in the fourth century. All of these writers acknowledge the right of persons to own property and to possess goods as their own. The issue has to do with how they use their possessions, especially what they do not need for meeting their own necessities. On this point Chrysostom states that "the rich are in possession of the goods of the poor, even if they have acquired them honestly or inherited them legally" (On Lazarus; Homily 11). He goes on to claim that the wealthy who do not share "are a species of bandit" (1 Corinthians; Homily 10:3).

For these early Christian writers the issue was not wealth or even the existence of poverty. The issue was how people of wealth related to those in need. As in the biblical understanding of justice, one's relationship with God was tied to one's relationship with other people, especially the poor and the marginalized. Failure to use one's possessions to help the needy was a failure to meet the expectations flowing from one's relationship with God. It was also a failure to recognize that whatever we own belongs to God and should be used to meet our needs and those of the larger community. All of these early church writings, especially the principle of the universal destination of the goods of creation, will have a shaping influence on modern Catholic social teachings.

Historical Developments

Throughout its history the church has endeavored to understand and live out what it means to be a follower of Jesus Christ in every age. To be a Christian carries expectations for how we live, not only in the most personal aspects of our lives, but also in the social contexts within which our lives unfold. These societies are in a constant state of change with new issues and new questions calling for answers. The biblical concern for the poor remained a pressing issue in early centuries. It has, in fact, continued as a critical concern in every period of the church's history, and is so today.

Other issues have lost their importance. Usury is such an example. Early Christian writers and medieval theologians alike condemned the lending of money with interest. Church councils from the twelfth to the fourteenth centuries condemned usury as did Thomas Aquinas (ST IIa IIae Q 66, a 7). Today the church's concern on this issue is not that lending money with interest is wrong, but that lending money with excessive interest is wrong. Slavery is another issue that receives quite a different response from the church today than during the patristic or early medieval periods. An earlier church made little effort to abolish slavery. Augustine among others regarded slavery as a consequence of original sin and as an unchangeable aspect of the economic system.

Many other social issues have been discussed and debated in every century. The morality of war, Christians' involvement in war, capital punishment, and church/state relations are examples. In every historical period certain topics of political or economic importance present themselves for public discussion. Church leaders often enter these public debates because the topics carry significant moral dimensions. Within the church there may be different positions taken on a particular topic, especially over several centuries. That is the case with usury and slavery. Even the issue of war has elicited multiple moral positions as both the just war theory and the pacifist stance have found support within the church's official teachings. All of this represents an effort by the living church to understand what it means in every historical period to be faithful to the demands of our relationship with Jesus Christ. The issues that bring this question to the forefront may change but the fundamental question remains the same.

The Beginnings

The nineteenth century marks the beginning of modern Catholic social teachings. As noted earlier, the church in every historical period sought to articulate moral teachings regarding contemporary issues. It was not until the late nineteenth century, however, that these teachings began to be written down in a systematic manner and presented as the official social teachings of the church. As always these teachings were responses to developments within society, especially in Europe. We can speculate on why they took the form of social encyclicals at this time. One reason undoubtedly was the fact that the events to which these teachings responded were having a major impact on the church itself.

Europe experienced a changing social order in the eighteenth and nineteenth centuries. On the social and political level, ideas from the Enlightenment fueled new ways of looking at the human person, the church, and society. Reason and the empirical sciences enjoyed an unprecedented respect. Individual rights, human freedom, religious tolerance and a firm belief in progress characterized social thought of the day. This thinking contributed to democratic movements throughout Europe and, eventually, to a changed political order. The most dramatic of these democratic movements, and one of the most violent, was the French Revolution (1789–99). This and other political revolutions of the time led to the suppression of the church in some countries as church property was confiscated and religious orders suppressed. The church's privileged position in society and its influence over ruling powers was greatly diminished as those powers increasingly were formed by democratic ideals.

On the economic side an equally powerful force for change was at work in the form of the Industrial Revolution. By the dawn of the nineteenth century it was clear that the economic structures in Europe and America were no longer those that the church had recognized and understood for so many generations. Gone were the self-sufficient artisan classes of the Middle Ages with their worker-protecting guild system. Replacing this system was a rising middle class and a mercantile system driven by a capitalist philosophy. In the wake of these economic changes the workers struggled for a decent livelihood as they often encountered low wages, long working hours, and unsafe working conditions.

The church's response to these developments—political and economic—tended to be defensive and reactionary. Its unhappy experience with the French Revolution left the Vatican suspicious of all political democratic movements. The church allied itself with conservative powers, especially monarchies, to stamp out liberal, democratic movements. Papal leadership recognized the hardships suffered by the working classes, but seemed unable to support needed economic reforms for fear such measures might lead to more social and political democratic changes. Throughout this period there were influential voices within the church calling for new thinking on the part of the papacy. As early as the 1820s, a Benedictine, Abbe Lamennais wrote that the church should align itself with the democratic movements.

> Let the Church support the democratic and revolutionary movement wherever it shows itself. Where the people are in arms against their rulers, let the Pope support them instead of their masters. The Church has everything to gain by the overthrow of the traditional political powers which hold her, as they hold the people. The natural alliance is that between the Pope and the people; the unnatural alliance which had cost the Church so dearly and had perverted its principles, was between the Pope and the King. (*L'Avenir*)

The papal response to such thinking as that represented by Lamennais can be seen in several encyclicals of the mid-nineteenth century. In his 1832 encyclical, *Mirari vos*, Pope Gregory XVI condemned the principles of separation of church and state, freedom of the press, freedom of religion, and freedom of conscience. His successor, Pius IX, issued an encyclical named *Quanta Cura* in 1864. This document contained the famous "Syllabus of Errors" which condemned liberal programs of modern democracy and even modern civilization (proposition 80).

A less defensive posture was struck by Bishop Wilhelm von Kettler of Mainz, Germany. Kettler, more than any other church leader, helped the church recognize the real nature of the nineteenth century economic and social issues. His many publications on the plight of workers during the industrialization of Europe helped to awaken within the church an urgency to speak out on behalf of the laboring classes. Kettler's influence on Pope Leo XIII is reflected in the pontiff's 1891 encyclical, On the

Condition of Labor *(Rerum Novarum)*—the first modern Catholic social document.

The Documents

Catholic social teachings come to us in a body of documents written by Pope Leo XIII and his successors up to the present moment. These include papal social encyclicals, council and synodical documents, as well as apostolic letters and exhortations. The number of documents is not large, about a dozen depending upon what one chooses to include in this body of official Catholic social documents. For purposes of this writing I am including all the papal documents contained in the publication by David O'Brien and Thomas Shannon, *Catholic Social Thought: The Documentary Heritage.* These include:

- On the Condition of Labor *(Rerum Novarum)* 1891, Leo XIII.
- On Reconstructing the Social Order *(Quadragesimo Anno)* 1931, Pius XI.
- Christianity and Social Progress *(Mater et Magistra)* 1961, John XXIII.
- Peace on Earth *(Pacem in Terris)* 1961, John XXIII.
- Pastoral Constitution on the Church in the Modern World *(Gaudium et Spes)* 1965, Vatican Council II.
- On the Development of Peoples *(Populorum Progressio)* 1967, Paul VI.
- A Call to Action *(Octogesima Adveniens)* 1971, Paul VI.
- Justice in the World *(Justicia in Mundo)* 1971, Synod of Bishops.
- Evangelization in the Modern World *(Evangelii Nuntiandi)* 1975, Paul VI.
- On Human Work *(Laborem Exercens)* 1981, John Paul II.
- On Social Concern *(Sollicitudo Rei Socialis)* 1987, John Paul II.
- On the Hundredth Anniversary of *Rerum Novarum (Centesimus Annus)* 1991, John Paul II.

The social documents seek to make a connection between Christian faith and the questions and challenges of contemporary society. They attempt to help bridge the split between the faith that we profess and our daily lives, a separation that the Second Vatican Council "counted among the more serious errors of our age" (The Church in the Modern

World, 43). In that sense Catholic social teachings lead us to recognize that our faith must show itself in our public life. It is a faith that spurs us into the struggle to build a society and a world that more closely reflects the love and mercy, the justice and peace of God.

These social teachings at the same time provide us with moral guidance in addressing particular problems confronting us in society. Each of these documents is to some extent a response to critical issues of its day. On the Condition of Labor (1891) speaks to the problems facing workers in the late nineteenth century. On the Development of Peoples (1967) confronts the challenges of global poverty and related development. On the Hundredth Anniversary of *Rerum Novarum* (1991) critiques capitalism and socialism after the fall of the socialist governments in Eastern Europe.

As they discuss issues of their day, these documents build upon the teachings of earlier social encyclicals. Running through this body of teachings is a set of moral principles and fundamental perspectives about the human person and the organization of society. The historically conditioned issues that the documents address may fade in importance over time. The moral themes and perspectives that have evolved from these documents are the enduring teachings.

In the mid-1990s the Catholic bishops of the United States identified seven "key themes that are at the heart of our Catholic social tradition." These themes provide a framework for considering the contents of the encyclicals and applying their wisdom to our contemporary lives. They are a starting point for engaging Catholic social teaching in order to live our faith today and build a more just society. Each of the following chapters explores one of these themes.

Chapter 2

Life and Dignity of the Human Person

At twenty-two years of age Stacey checked herself into a chemical treatment program. After a ten-year addiction to methamphetamine and alcohol, this single mother of two children knew her life must change or it would end soon. Stacey could point to any number of reasons for her sad condition—raised in a family with a chemical dependency history, herself a victim of sexual abuse, she made too many bad choices along the way. Whatever was in her past, Stacey knew that her own treatment was necessary for her children's future. A successful treatment program was the beginning of a new life not only for her daughters, but also for Stacey herself. In the years since treatment she has discovered that nurturing her spiritual growth is an essential part of her life. She is a person who appreciates the journey she is on, a woman with self-confidence and restored dignity. Today she works in an addictions recovery program helping other people to realize that they can change, that they can become the persons God created them to be.

&co;

Human Dignity

The dignity of the human person is the foundation of all Catholic social teaching. It underlies the claim that human life is sacred and that every one of us, like Stacey, has the ability to live life to the fullest. Human dignity also is the starting point for understanding what this teaching says about social, economic, and political topics—about human life in organized society. Within the social documents are several key points about human dignity.

Our relationship with God

In the history of Christian theology we find different ways of explaining human dignity. Through much of this history the favored explanation rested on the claim that humans alone possess the gifts of intellect and will; in this way do we bear a likeness to God and therefore a sacred dignity. St. Thomas Aquinas developed this argument in his *Summa Theologica*.

For modern Catholic social teaching the most important aspect of human dignity is what it reveals about our relationship with God. The first creation story in the Book of Genesis states that men and women are made in the image of God (Gen 1:26). The biblical account does not provide an explanation of what it means to be made in God's image except for one obvious fact: humans enjoy a very special relationship with the Creator. Man and woman alone—among all of God's creatures—were made "in the likeness of God." This biblical idea is central to Catholic social teaching on the dignity of the human person and the consequent sacredness of human life.

At the end of its final session the Second Vatican Council gave us the beautiful Pastoral Constitution on the Church in the Modern World (1965). This document provides the broadest discussion of human dignity to be found in the social teachings. It answers two critical questions: what do we mean by human dignity and what are its implications for Christian living. Speaking about the equality of all people, The Church in the Modern World asserts:

> Since all men possess a rational soul and are created in God's likeness, since they have the same nature and origin, have been redeemed by Christ, and enjoy the same divine calling and destiny, the basic equality of all must receive increasingly greater recognition. (29)

Addressing the specific question of why we claim such dignity for humans, this special status among God's creatures, the document states that "an outstanding cause of human dignity lies in man's call to communion with God" (19). This dignity rests on the fact that we are created by God's love and called to be with our Creator forever. Our life is a vocation, but one with a clear communitarian dimension. "For having been created in the image of God . . . all men are called to one and the same goal, namely, God himself. For this reason love for God and neighbor is the first and greatest commandment. Sacred scripture, however, teaches us that the love of God cannot be separated from love of neighbor" (24).

A summary of this teaching on human dignity is that we are created by God, redeemed by Christ and called to communion with God. Our recognition that every human being shares in this dignity—in this special relationship with the Creator—leads us to the second key point about human dignity in Catholic social teachings.

Our gift to the neighbor

Human dignity includes a recognition that every person enjoys this special relationship with our Creator—created, redeemed, called. In this we acknowledge as well that we share a special relationship with one another. All of this is captured so beautifully yet simply in the great commandment: love of God and love of neighbor. The Church in the Modern World points out that a person "cannot fully find himself except through a sincere gift of himself" (24). Our relationship with one another is grounded in this shared dignity and is fully realized as we contribute to one another's journey to the Creator.

Catholic social teaching consistently underscores the social nature of humans, a point to be developed in the next chapter. For now it is worth noting that this social nature is at the very core of our understanding of human dignity. Made in the image of God, humans are able to reflect the loving and life-giving relationship we associate with God. We are able to enter into loving relationships with one another, relationships in which we genuinely seek the good of the other person. The Vatican II document insists that we cannot fully realize our dignity unless we accept such a stance towards our neighbor. "For by his innermost nature man is a social being, and unless he relates himself to others he can neither live nor develop his potentials" (12). Our social nature and our growing awareness of our dignity direct us towards God and towards others (The Church in the Modern World, 31). Human dignity, this wonderful gift from our Creator, is anything but a gift to be enjoyed in isolation from others. It has as much to do with who we are and where we are headed as it does with how we relate to other people along the way. It also imposes responsibility for our own development.

Taking responsibility for our lives

If human dignity suggests that all of us are called to communion with God then every one of us has a responsibility to let that happen. Pope Paul VI, in his 1967 encyclical, On the Development of Peoples, addressed that obligation in the language of personal responsibility and vocation.

> In the design of God, every man is called upon to develop and fulfill himself, for every life is a vocation. At birth, everyone is granted, in germ, a set of aptitudes and qualities for him to bring to fruition. (15)

We do this through our entire lives. Our personal relationships, the formative years in our families, our education, our work—all of this provides the context within which we respond to this vocation, to this calling from our Creator. It is in and through these evolving stages of life that we are granted the opportunities to develop and to bring to fruition the gifts and talents that God has granted. Stacey is using her gifts to help other people change their lives, something that would not have been possible if she had not taken responsibility for her own life and set it on a new course. As Paul VI states, each of us is responsible for our development, each of us must direct ourselves toward the destiny intended for us by our Creator. Though each person may be aided or impeded by his education and by other people around him, nonetheless "each one remains, whatever be these influences affecting him, the principal agent of his own success or failure" (15).

This accent on personal responsibility is tempered by the presumption within Catholic social teaching that moral responsibility requires sufficient freedom to choose and to act. That presumption is articulated most clearly in The Church in the Modern World, which tells us that freedom is necessary for persons to make the choices that lead them to their calling, the choices that direct them toward goodness.

> For its part, authentic freedom is an exceptional sign of the divine image within man. For God has willed that man be left "in the hand of his own counsel" (Sirach 15:14) so that he can seek his Creator

spontaneously, and come freely to utter and blissful perfection through loyalty to him. Hence, man's dignity demands that he act according to a knowing and free choice. (17)

This discussion of freedom and responsibility did not begin with the social teachings. Catholic moral theology always has recognized that each of us is responsible for the choices we make in life, for developing ourselves as followers of Jesus Christ. This tradition also has recognized that moral responsibility depends upon the freedom necessary for a person to know clearly the nature of the choices before him. Within the teaching is the notion of diminished responsibility suggesting that a person's physical, mental, or psychological state may be such as to lessen the moral responsibility associated with his actions. This is the theological background against which Pope Paul VI and the Second Vatican Council discuss responsibility and freedom. It is also the reference point for the claim in Catholic social teaching that social, economic, and political conditions can obstruct the realization of human dignity.

Life settings make a difference

The impact of social conditions upon a person's ability to grow and utilize her talents and to respond to God's call always has been recognized in Catholic social teaching. One might argue that this recognition necessitated the teachings. Nowhere in the documents is this topic discussed with more clarity and force than in The Church in the Modern World.

> Now a man can scarcely arrive at the needed sense of responsibility unless his living conditions allow him to become conscious of his dignity, and to rise to his destiny by spending himself for God and for others. But human freedom is often crippled when a man falls into extreme poverty, just as it withers when he indulges in too many of life's comforts and imprisons himself in a kind of splendid isolation. (31)

One's living conditions can allow or prevent a person from exercising responsibility for her life and directing that life to the service of God and neighbor. Those living conditions may be serious poverty or excessive indulgence in material possessions, either of which can prevent a person from realizing how great is his dignity. Either of these conditions can hinder a person from living out the expectations of one's relationship with God and neighbor.

This point is reiterated when the same document explores various aspects of economic life. In this instance the concern is for persons living in poverty.

> While an enormous mass of people still lacks the absolute necessities of life, some, even in less advanced countries, live sumptuously or squander wealth. Luxury and misery rub shoulders. While the few enjoy very great freedom of choice, the many are deprived of almost all possibility of acting on their own initiative and responsibility, and often subsist in living and working conditions unworthy of human beings. (63)

The realization of human dignity requires at minimum that people enjoy the basic necessities of life. Without them people have very little hope of acting with the freedom and responsibility expected of persons created by God, redeemed by Christ, and called to communion with God. The scandal of poverty and oppression is the failure of those who are rich and powerful to recognize the sacred dignity of those who are not. It is the failure of all of us to assist each of us in becoming the person God intended through his loving creation.

Developing the whole person

Helping people to meet their basic economic necessities is a first step to honoring the sacredness of human life. It is, however, only a beginning. All human beings are called by God to develop themselves fully, to utilize all their talents and gifts, to place themselves at the service of others. This vision of the human vocation invites us to appreciate all that is needed for full human development. This vision led Pope Paul VI to introduce to Catholic social teaching the notion of integral development. "Development cannot be limited to mere economic growth. In order for it to be authentic, it must be complete: integral, that is, it has to promote the good of every man and of the whole man" (On the Development of Peoples, 14).

This document also points to a connection between improved material conditions and the development of the human spirit. While cautioning against a form of development that is focused principally on material prosperity, Paul VI also notes: "Not that material prosperity of itself precludes the activity of the human spirit. On the contrary, the human spirit, 'increasingly free of its bondage to creatures, can be more easily drawn to the worship and contemplation of the Creator'" (41). As a person's most basic material needs are met that person is able to direct attention to other needs. Once free of a survival mode of existence, such as economic poverty or chemical dependency, people can more easily attend to social, psychological, and spiritual needs. This leads to the total, integral human development that Pope Paul VI presented, a development that includes spiritual growth.

From this perspective, to work for a more just society and to struggle against poverty anywhere is to encourage the full, integral development of all humankind.

> To wage war on misery and to struggle against injustice is to promote, along with improved conditions, the human and spiritual progress of all men, and therefore the common good of humanity. (On the Development of Peoples, 76)

Embracing our dignity

Catholic social documents offer a broad picture of the meaning of human dignity. These writings also make the case that the dignity of the human person is at the very core of who we are, especially regarding our relationship with God and with one another. In the second half of the twentieth century these teachings begin to note the rising public awareness of human dignity.

Pope John XXIII, in Peace on Earth (1963) observes three distinctive characteristics of his age: workers are gaining ground in both economic and public affairs, colonized nations are gaining independence, and women are taking part in public life.

> Since women are becoming ever more conscious of their human dignity, they will not tolerate being treated as mere material instruments, but demand rights befitting a human person both in domestic and in public life. (41)

In that discussion John XXIII encourages people to move forward, to see the connection between their dignity and basic human rights. He states that a person "who possesses certain rights has likewise the duty to claim those rights as marks of his dignity" (44). An even stronger acknowledgement that people are more and more aware of their dignity comes from Pope Paul VI's apostolic letter, A Call to Action (1971). He notes the remarkable progress in scientific and technological developments that impact so many aspects of modern life. Yet in these new contexts, two human aspirations grow stronger and more visible: "the aspiration to equality and the aspiration to participation, two forms of man's dignity and freedom" (22). This desire for equality and the desire to participate in social, economic, and political areas of life reflect the basic human longing for freedom. That is the freedom necessary to exercise responsibility for one's life, to direct one's life towards the end intended by the Creator. That is the freedom necessary to realize human dignity.

Threats to Human Dignity Today

In every place and in every age human life and the dignity of the human person have come under attack. Some of these threats are unique to a certain historical period, some to a particular part of the globe. Many of these threats to human dignity transcend time and place and have followed human history from its inception. This is a part of the human condition, a consequence of human sin, an ongoing tragic reality of our existence. Threats to human life and dignity take many forms. Some represent direct attacks upon human life, others have the character of diminishing the quality of life, as with Stacey's past addiction. The latter will be discussed in chapter 3. Here our attention is on those threats which Catholic social teaching considers as direct attacks upon life.

Abortion

It is hardly a revelation to state that Catholic teaching regards abortion as a morally unjustifiable act. This position of the institutional church is widely known and is summarized by the U.S. Catholic bishops in their 2004 pastoral statement, Faithful Citizenship: "Abortion, the deliberate killing of a human being before birth, is never morally acceptable" (17). This teaching rests on the belief that human life begins at the moment of conception. Thus, neither late- nor early-term abortions can be justified since a human being is present from conception through every stage of the pregnancy. The church's teaching reminds us that every human life enjoys a sacred dignity because each life is created in God's image, redeemed by God's love in Christ, and called to communion with God.

The practical implications of this theology are clear. Catholics should not have, support, or in any way encourage abortions. With equal clarity this teaching calls us to defend the life and dignity of every human being, from conception through natural death. What is less clear is how Catholics should endeavor to stop or limit abortions within the United States. The Supreme Court decision of 1973 *(Roe v. Wade)* legalized abortions through the first trimester and today in the United States there are around one million abortions each year. Clearly, Catholic teaching regards these as unjustifiable direct attacks upon human life.

A challenge for Catholics in the United States is to discern how to prevent or limit these abortions in a society where public opinion polls indicate that the vast majority of citizens do not want to re-criminalize abortion. Working to make abortions illegal might not be the best and certainly not the only way to limit their occurrence in this society. One of the criteria for good law according to Catholic moral theology is that the law must be enforceable. Even if a law were passed to outlaw abortion, its enforceability would be questionable in the absence of a social consensus supporting its enactment. Any effort to end abortion through legislative procedures should be built upon prior efforts to develop that necessary consensus. In addition, we would do well to explore whether there are particular social or economic factors that contribute to some people choosing abortions.

Assisted suicide and euthanasia

Assisted suicide and euthanasia are further examples of unjustifiable assaults on human life. Helping someone to end her own life or directly putting an end to the life of someone because that person is handicapped, sick, or even dying (euthanasia) is a denial of the dignity and sacredness of that person's life. Even when these actions are carried out for good motives, such as the desire to end a person's suffering, the direct and intentional ending of a human life is wrong. As Faithful Citizenship notes, "The purposeful taking of a human life by assisted suicide and euthanasia is never an act of mercy" (17).

Euthanasia is not the same as foregoing extraordinary medical procedures that are disproportionate to the expected outcome and that may cause a financial burden to family members. Nor should euthanasia be confused with the discontinuance of medically administered nutrition and hydration. The latter may be morally appropriate when death is immanent or when the technology is ineffective or excessively burdensome to patient or to family members. The decision to withhold such medical procedures is not an action that causes death but an acceptance that death is immanent. As medical sciences advance the profession's ability to extend life, questions arise regarding the quality of the life being extended. Moral theology related to medical ethics as well as Catholic social teaching direct us to assess these situations in light of our belief in the dignity of humans and how the sanctity of life is best protected.

Embryonic stem cell research

Recent advances in the science of molecular biology have created dramatically new possibilities for improving human life in this century. Genetic engineering related to food production, medical care, and human reproduction are three of the better known examples. While these developments offer enormous potential for improving human life, each of them presents risks and raises ethical questions.

The greatest concern to Catholic moral theology coming from these developments is the use of human embryos in stem cell research. Some of this research is aimed at improvements in medical care, offering new hope for cures to old diseases. Other work is intended to bring new possibilities in human reproduction, including the cloning of human beings. Whatever the motive behind such research, if it involves the use of live human embryos as a supply source for stem cells, the actions or procedures cannot be morally justified. Such procedures involve the destruction of human embryos which represent living human beings. As with abortion, this destruction of unborn human lives is always wrong.

Death penalty

Capital punishment represents yet another direct threat against human life. With more than three thousand persons on death row in 2005, the United States remains one of the few industrialized nations that allows use of the death penalty. On a visit to the United States in 1999 Pope John Paul II declared capital punishment to be both cruel and unnecessary (Homily, St. Louis, Jan. 27). Five years later the U.S. Catholic bishops wrote that "our nation's increasing reliance on the death penalty cannot be justified" (Faithful Citizenship, 19). Killing those who kill is no way to teach that killing is wrong. More violence is not the answer to violence. The bishops stated that this stand against the death penalty is part of the church's pro-life commitment.

In his encyclical, The Gospel of Life, Pope John Paul II provided a clear statement of the church's position on capital punishment. He noted approvingly the growing tendency throughout the world to limit the use of capital punishment or to abolish it altogether. He acknowledged that the punishment of offenders has a legitimate purpose—to defend public order, ensure public safety, and provide the offender "an incentive to change and be rehabilitated." The latter may be difficult if the punishment used is the death penalty. One of the problems with the death penalty from a Catholic perspective is that this ultimate form of punishment not only limits or ends the offender's life, but it also limits the possibility of the offender accepting God's call to conversion. The death penalty ends the possibility of God's grace moving the offender to a change of heart. It is fundamentally an act against hope.

The Gospel of Life acknowledges what the traditional teaching of the church has long held, that the state may legitimately use the death penalty if this is the only possible way to protect citizens against an unjust aggressor.

> The nature and extent of the punishment ought not to go to the extreme of executing the offender, except in cases of absolute necessity: in other words, when it would not be possible otherwise to defend society. Today, however, as a result of steady improvements in the organization of the penal system, such cases are very rare if not practically nonexistent. (56)

The last sentence suggests that while it is theoretically possible for a situation in which use of the death penalty is morally justified, in practice it is not so. Certainly it is the case that in countries with advanced penal justice systems such as is present in the United States, the death penalty is not needed to protect citizens and therefore cannot be morally justified.

One final point should be noted regarding the church's social teaching on the death penalty. The church's stance against the use of capital punishment is grounded in the dignity of the human person. That special status is granted by God. We do not lose or forfeit our dignity by sinning, not even by committing horrendous acts against other people. In Christian hope we believe in the possibility of conversion of even the most hardened criminal on death row. We believe that God's love and mercy is ever present in spite of our foolish and sometimes terrible actions. The church's position is to defend human life—every human life—from conception to natural death. The stance against both abortion and the death penalty is grounded on the sacred dignity of the human person. It is not about innocent life or guilty life, but human life.

War

A final threat to human dignity that needs to be recognized in our day is war. Catholic social teaching recognizes that a nation has the right to defend itself against unjust aggression. In this day such aggression often comes in the form of terrorist attacks. The tragedy of 9/11 marked a high point in such direct attacks upon innocent people that have been conducted over many decades in different parts of the world. We may acknowledge how economic inequality, destitution, and even political policies contribute to the sense of hopelessness that gives rise to desperate acts. At the same time, we must recognize the immoral character of any act of violence intended to harm or kill innocent human beings, regardless of motives. Because their objective is to frighten and kill civilians, terrorist actions have always been regarded by Catholic social teaching as unjustifiable assaults on human life. They are always wrong.

Nations, however, have a right to protect themselves against attacks whether from other nations or from shadowy groups intent on spreading violence and destruction. The Second Vatican Council upheld this right of a nation to self-defense. "As long as the danger of war remains and there is no competent and sufficiently powerful authority at the international level, governments cannot be denied the right to legitimate defense once every means of peaceful settlement has been exhausted" (The Church in the Modern World, 79).

While legitimate right to self-defense is recognized, it is important to see that any discussion on this topic in Catholic social teaching begins with a presumption against war. This stance is grounded in the fundamental Christian commandment to love one another and to do no harm to our neighbor. The U.S. Catholic bishops' 1983 pastoral letter, The Challenge of Peace: God's Promise and Our Response, summarizes this position well.

> The Church's teaching on war and peace establishes a strong presumption against war which is binding on all; it then examines when this presumption may be overridden, precisely in the name of preserving the kind of peace which protects human dignity and human rights. (70)

The pastoral later observes that the possibility of taking even one human life—even that of an enemy—"is a prospect we should consider in fear and trembling" (80).

The bishops then ask how it is possible to move from this presumption against war to a justifiable use of lethal force? Their answer is in the centuries-old just war criteria. Serious questions may be raised today regarding the practicality of these criteria in the twenty-first century. As long as they remain the moral guidelines for discerning the moral justification for going to war, one important point merits emphasis. The just war criteria are intended to prevent war, not to help us find moral justification for entering a war to which we are already committed. They establish strong conditions that must be met for setting aside the presumption against war. Among these conditions or criteria we find just cause (the war is only to confront a real and certain danger), last resort (all peaceful alternatives must have been exhausted), and proportionality (the damage to be inflicted and the costs incurred by the war must be proportionate to the good expected by taking up arms).

These concerns were among the reasons for both the Vatican and the U.S. Catholic bishops firmly declaring in 2003 that the expected American attack against Iraq appeared unjustifiable. In 2004, long after the war had commenced, the bishops again stated: "While military force as a last resort can sometimes be justified against aggression and similar threats to the common good, we have raised serious moral concerns and questions about preemptive or preventive use of force" (Faithful Citizenship, 19).

War in our day increasingly resembles a direct attack against life. Civil wars in African nations claim millions of noncombatants as their victims. In the Middle East, responses to terrorist attacks too often fail to discriminate between perpetrators of violence and innocent citizens. In spite of strategic bombing technologies, the U.S.-led war in Iraq has left tens of thousands of Iraqi civilians dead. People in any of these war zones die in the daily cross-fire between the technologically sophisticated weaponry of government forces and the crude killing devices of insurgents and terrorists. For these civilians it is difficult to experience the conflict as anything but an attack or at least a threat against their most basic right—to continue living.

Defending Human Dignity

Human dignity is the basis for claiming all human life to be sacred. It is at the core of our understanding of the human person—her unique relationship to God, her special place within creation, her vocation as communion with God. Respecting the dignity of every person is a precondition for a peaceful and healthy human community.

The burden of defending human life and dignity rests upon society as a whole, including government. The measure of every institution, program, policy, and system is whether it threatens or enhances the life and dignity of every person within that society. This is simultaneously a call to defend life as well as the means necessary to live that life with dignity. To do so is to promote human progress and the full development of all people (On the Development of Peoples, 76). It is to work for the common good of every society and of all humanity. It is to build a world wherein everyone can live a fully human life. This defense of life and dignity is not one issue but a broad task.

> It is not just a matter of eliminating hunger, or even of reducing poverty. The struggle against destitution, though urgent and necessary, is not enough. It is a question, rather, of building a world where every man, no matter what his race, religion, or nationality, can live a fully human life, freed from servitude imposed on him by other men or by natural forces over which he has not sufficient control. (On the Development of Peoples, 47)

The primary responsibility of defending human dignity rests upon every member of society. The Second Vatican Council underscored the point that each of us is responsible for one another.

> [E]veryone must consider his very neighbor without exception as another self, taking into account first of all his life and the means necessary to living it with dignity, so as not to imitate the rich man who had no concern for the poor Lazarus. (The Church in the Modern World, 27)

A striking aspect of this statement is the unsettling assertion that each and every one of us has the power and the means to defend the dignity of other people. This responsibility does not rest solely on government or on leaders of the community. Each of us can do something; each of us has a Lazarus relationship.

Discussion

1. Name one special gift or talent God has given you that you can use for the benefit of the larger community.

2. Can you identify anyone (family member, friend, acquaintance) who, like Stacey, has made major changes in her or his life and is now helping others?

3. Besides the legislative process, what are some other ways to help decrease the number of abortions in the United States?

4. How would you explain to someone why the church takes a stand against use of the death penalty?

Actions

1. Visit a social service provider (County Social Services, Catholic Charities) and ask this person what are some social or economic factors that play a role in some persons choosing abortion. How might we address these factors?

2. Talk with a refugee who has fled his or her country because of war, terrorism or other forms of violence. What does this tell you about war?

3. What programs or activities does your parish have that support human dignity?

Chapter 3

Call to Family, Community, and Participation

Aaron recently retired from his job at a local optical manufacturing plant. With more time available he has increased his volunteer hours at a homeless shelter, something he has been doing most of his adult life. Aaron volunteers for a number of reasons: he enjoys the social contact, he believes it is one practical way to live out Christ's command to love our neighbor, and he thinks every citizen should do something extra to make our communities better. This is his extra something, though it does not end with his service at the homeless shelter. In recent years Aaron has combined his service at the shelter with political advocacy at the state legislature, trying to bring needed changes in programs and public policies affecting persons who are homeless.

☙❧

Community/Society

Catholic social teaching tells us that all persons are social by nature. We grow and develop in various forms of community—family, school, church, work, recreation, volunteering. Though some of us may be more introverted than others, we nonetheless depend upon our social relationships for a necessary and healthy maturing as responsible persons. Despite the popularity of self-help programs as well as the cultural enshrinement of individualism, it remains true that humans grow and achieve fulfillment in community. Aaron's reaching out to serve the homeless in service and justice actions is not simply about helping others. His volunteering also is a necessary part of his own development.

The social relationships that we forge and the contexts in which we live and work are important to our development. Our workplace environment, our relationships in school, even the health of our families can impact that development. It is also true that how we organize society—in economics, politics, law—directly affects the realization of human dignity and the capacity of individuals to grow in community. Income, health care, housing—all of these play a role in determining how each person progresses in economic, social, cultural, and spiritual ways. How a society attends to these critical areas of human need has a bearing on how individuals fare in their total human development.

All contribute to the common good

Each of us lives in society and draws countless benefits from our social settings. This is one of many reasons why we in turn should do everything we can to make our communities as healthy and strong as possible. It is up to every citizen to shape these communities—and society as a whole—as places where human dignity is respected and where every person can find what is needed to follow his or her vocation. The Church in the Modern World makes this point: "Citizens, for their part, should remember that they have the right and the duty, which must be recognized by civil authority, to contribute according to their ability to the true progress of their community" (65). There are many ways to make that contribution. We do so through our jobs, volunteering, paying taxes, contributing to charities, becoming politically active. Each of us has particular talents, gifts, and abilities given by our Creator to meet our own needs and to help build up the larger community. Jesus' call to love our neighbor is a call to us as individuals, but as individuals in community. This biblical commandment has a social dimension.

In Catholic social teaching this communal dimension of the great commandment often takes the language of contributing to the common good. Pope John XXIII (Christianity and Social Progress, 65) as well as the Second Vatican Council define the common good as including all areas of life:

> Now, the common good embraces the sum of those conditions of social life by which individuals, families, and groups can achieve their own fulfillment in a relatively thorough and ready way. (The Church in the Modern World, 74)

The Council underlined the importance of moving beyond a purely individualistic ethic in defining both our relationship to the larger society and our obligations as Christians.

> Profound and rapid changes make it particularly urgent that no one, ignoring the trend of events or drugged by laziness, content himself with a merely individualistic morality. (30)

Rather, our responsibilities as Christians, our duties to justice and love, can be fulfilled most effectively by looking outward, by making our contribution to those agencies and organizations committed to improving human life. Our own abilities and the needs of others will determine the nature of that contribution.

This accent on the common good in Catholic social teaching counters the ever-present temptation to seek only one's own good within society, to support those changes in public policies and programs (such as taxes, welfare, education) that benefit oneself personally. A consequence of living in a "common good morality" is that we must bring our "own interests into harmony with the needs of the community" (Peace on Earth, 53). In this respect it is worth noting that private ownership, which Catholic social teaching always has upheld, is not an unqualified right. Our use of whatever we own must be guided by a respect for our neighbors and the needs of the larger society. The controversies regarding large-scale livestock facilities in rural communities illustrate the challenge of balancing private interests with community rights and needs.

Citizens may contribute to the common good through a more active engagement in the governance of society. If we are to do that well, then we need to be formed and educated on how our society functions and on how we personally may contribute to its well-being, especially in its political dimensions. The Second Vatican Council stated that civic and political education is "supremely necessary" so that "all citizens can make their contribution to the political community" (The Church in the Modern World, 75). In that same discussion the Council specifically noted that voting is not only a right and duty; it is a way of promoting the common good.

Church members

Catholic social teaching holds that Christians especially have reason to work for the betterment of society. A defining expectation of Christians—love of neighbor—must find expression in the practical acts within the social context. In their 1971 statement, *Justice in the World*, the Synod of Bishops asserted that members of the church share with other members of society the right and duty to promote the common good. In fact, it is an even stronger duty. "Christians ought to fulfill their temporal obligations with fidelity and competence. They should act as a leaven in the world, in their family, professional, social, cultural and political life" (38). In all areas of life Christians have the opportunity to put their faith, their hope, and their love into effective action. We carry out our jobs, look after our families, and volunteer within our communities not because these are burdensome obligations. We do these activities because these are the ordinary, practical ways of following Christ's command to love one another. They also provide us with a means of checking on a daily basis if we are living in fidelity to the expectations of our relationships—with God, with one another, and with all of creation.

In the political organization and functioning of society, Christians find another occasion for making this contribution. *The Church in the Modern World* speaks of Christians having a specific and proper role in the political community. In living out this role Christians should set a clear example "of devotion to the sense of duty and of service to the advancement of the common good" (75). Our Christian identity of loving and caring for our neighbor takes visible form in our political efforts to build a more just society, much as it does in Aaron's work for legislative changes on behalf of homeless persons.

Government's role

In the United States today there is much discussion and debate about the role of government. Depending upon religious or philosophical views, people argue for either a greater or lesser place for government in promoting the common good. Some of this discussion relates to taxation and differing views on how much of citizens' earned income should be given to the government to do its job. In the end this comes down to how we answer the question: what is the purpose of government?

In the Catholic moral tradition government has a limited but significant role to play. Its very reason for existence is the realization of the common good—to help bring about "those conditions of social life by which individuals, families, and groups can achieve their own fulfillment in a relatively thorough and ready way" (*The Church in the Modern World*, 74). The U.S. Catholic bishops speak of this as a moral function of government—protecting human rights and securing basic justice for all members of society.

> Society as a whole and in all its diversity is responsible for building
> up the common good. But it is the government's role to guarantee
> the minimum conditions that make this rich social activity possible,
> namely, human rights and justice. (Economic Justice for All, 122)

In 1971 Pope Paul VI spoke of this role of government, of using political power to create "the conditions required for attaining man's true and
complete good, including his spiritual end" (A Call to Action, 46). Note
that this is not a call for government to involve itself in religious or
spiritual matters, but for government to help create the conditions that
allow for the spiritual dimension of human growth. The principle of
subsidiarity cautions against any level of government doing what individuals or smaller entities can do for themselves. Rather, it is the task of
government to create the conditions and to help smaller units carry out
their own responsibilities.

Nonetheless, Catholic social teaching recognizes an additional function
of civil authorities, a function or responsibility that locates itself within
the broader task of promoting the common good. "Considerations of
justice and equity, however, can at times demand that those involved in
civil government give more attention to the less fortunate members of
the community, since they are less able to defend their rights and to assert
their legitimate claims" (Peace on Earth, 56).

An earlier document by Pope Pius XI, On Reconstructing the Social
Order (1931) spoke of this same function of government in the context
of respecting the roles of other entities within society.

> It is true, indeed, that requisite freedom of action must be left to
> individual citizens and families; but this should be with due regard
> for the common good and with no injury to anyone. It is the duty
> of rulers to protect the community and its various parts, but in pro-
> tecting the rights of individuals they must have special regard for
> the infirm and needy. (25)

John XXIII expanded this particular concern of government to include
the weaker members of society such as workers, women, and children.
The Pope added that the government must never "neglect its duty to
contribute actively to the betterment of the living conditions of workers"
(Christianity and Social Progress, 20).

Catholic social teaching holds that a special purpose of ruling authorities is to look after the poor and the vulnerable, and to ensure that their

basic needs are met and rights respected. This is part of the government's responsibility to promote the common good. Society as a whole cannot do well if its weakest members are hurting. None of this suggests that individuals and religious bodies have no role in helping the poor and the powerless. All of us are called to respond to anyone in need. This teaching on the role of government, however, underscores the claim that the satisfaction of human rights and basic human needs cannot be left to charity alone. It is the responsibility of government to meet these needs when they are not being met by private or communal charity. For any government to meet its responsibility in this matter it must be provided needed financial resources, most commonly through taxes. Catholic social teaching sees little value in general pledges to not raise taxes. Any discussion about appropriate levels of taxation must be grounded upon a prior discernment of needs.

Politics

One of the interesting developments in the 110 plus years of modern Catholic social statements is the increasing attention directed towards the field of politics. In the earliest documents—those by Popes Leo XIII and Pius XI—much was said about the role of government but very little about politics. Even less was stated regarding the ordinary citizen's role in politics. That changed after the Second Vatican Council.

In 1971 Pope Paul VI wrote his apostolic letter, A Call to Action. As the title suggests, Paul VI was calling all Christians to become active in social justice efforts. One arena for such activity is politics. Noting the "radical limitation to economics," the Pope acknowledged the need "to pass from economics to politics" (46). He pointed out that decisions made by those holding political power influence all areas of community life, especially the social and economic fields. Politics involves concrete realities and choices to be made on behalf of the public good. It is in making those choices, through political activity, that all of us bring our values to bear on the common good.

Politics, then, can be a way of "living the Christian commitment to the service of others" (46). Aaron's volunteering at the shelter has made him more aware of the needs of homeless persons. That awareness has led him to engage in social justice actions to bring about needed changes in programs and services for persons in need. This is political action on Aaron's part and a witness to the Christian's call to service and change, to charity and justice.

Politics is a form of service to others, a way of ensuring those conditions of social life that make it possible for all citizens to achieve their own fulfillment. Whether ordinary citizens or professional politicians, all of us are social beings with a responsibility to take part in the organization and life of political society. Choosing legislative representatives and shaping public opinion is a necessary part of our shared social life. Both citizens and professional politicians must be focused upon what is needed by the larger society. In an era when individualism and extreme partisanship crowd out genuine efforts to improve society, it is good to recall that even political parties "should never prefer their own advantage over this same common good" (The Church in the Modern World, 75).

Universal common good

Catholic social teaching encourages all of us to take an active role in public life, to engage in the political realm to the extent our abilities, interests, and state in life allow. This is a significant way for us to contribute to the building of a healthy society. At the same time, this working for the common good must take on a universal character. It must not be confined to the boundaries of our own community, state, or even nation. The Church in the Modern World makes the case.

> Every day, human interdependence grows more tightly drawn and spreads by degrees over the whole world. As a result the common good . . . today takes on an increasingly universal complexion and consequently involves rights and duties with respect to the whole human race. Every social group must take account of the needs and legitimate aspirations of other groups, and even of the general welfare of the entire human family. (26)

Whatever the issue at hand, nations must consider the effects of their decisions upon other nations, a point made by the U.S. Catholic bishops in Global Climate Change regarding this government's response: "Responses to global climate change should reflect our interdependence and common responsibility for the future of our planet. Individual nations must measure their own self-interest against the greater common good and contribute equitably to global solutions" (8).

A balance is needed also between patriotic support for one's country and a loving concern for people of other nations. Patriotism should not lead to a nationalistic narrow-mindedness that is incapable of genuinely considering the welfare of the entire human family.

Finally, the universal common good, like the common good of an individual nation, may require an appropriate governing body to ensure its realization. Pope John XXIII addressed this need when he wrote in Peace on Earth that because the universal common good presents problems that go beyond national boundaries, there is need for a "public authority which is in a position to operate in an effective manner on a world-wide basis. The moral order itself . . . demands that such a form of public authority be established" (137). Later Catholic social documents repeated this call for a "universal public authority," such as the United Nations, as the only sure way to outlaw war (The Church in the Modern World, 83) and to promote global development (On the Development of Peoples, 76).

Family

As a social being the human person lives, works, and develops in the midst of other people. Each of us, if we are to grow into morally responsible persons, must learn to get along with others, to look out for one another, and to cooperate in building healthy communities. The learning process that leads to this socially responsible living begins in the family. The church always has taught that the family is the central social institution, the basic cell of human society (Peace on Earth, 16). If the family is so important to society, then society must maintain an environment in which families can flourish. Among other concerns, every nation and culture must be clear on the relationship between marriage and family life, on the need for adequate family income, and on the kind of education that families provide.

The family

The family is so important to society because it is in the family that we learn who we are and how we are to relate to others. It is in the family that most of us learn that we are loved and that we are capable of loving others. All the virtues we need for responsible social living begin their development within our families. Catholic teaching believes that each of us finds our true identity in our social settings, in the give-and-take of our interactions with other people at work, worship, recreation, and in all the activities of daily living. The family plays a fundamental role in learning how to do all of this well, in providing the support needed to live each day in a way reflective of our sacred dignity and our vocation.

This connection between family life and life in society is made repeatedly in Catholic social documents. Pope John Paul II states that if we hope to overcome the individualistic mentality so characteristic of our era, then each of us needs to make a "concrete commitment to solidarity and charity," a commitment that begins in the family (On the Hundredth Anniversary, 49). The U.S. Catholic bishops, in their document, Communities of Salt and Light, remind us that the faith life nurtured in the family context touches all areas of our lives. "Our parishes need to encourage, support and sustain lay people in living their faith in the family, neighborhood, marketplace, and public arena."

The family is the central social institution, the basic cell of human society. A healthy family provides its members with opportunities to live their faith in the daily give-and-take of related and dependent social beings. It is in the family that children begin to learn the meaning of service, of looking beyond themselves, of reaching out to persons in need. This basic lesson, practiced daily and taken on as a good habit, leads family members to live as responsible, contributing members of society. Aaron's generosity in giving his time to the shelter for homeless persons did not originate in a vacuum. It grew from his own experience of family members loving and caring for him, and from their expectation that he would do likewise. The family is the primary agent of our education and formation.

Marriage

Catholic teaching on marriage is closely aligned with the church's understanding of family life. The institution of marriage and the raising of children in a family setting are difficult to separate. Modern documents acknowledge that one of the ends or values of marriage is the good of the spouses. Yet a second value of marriage continues to receive most of the attention in this day when the definition of marriage is under debate. That is the transmission of life, or in the language of past statements, the procreation and education of children. Most recently the U.S. Catholic bishops attempted to clarify how the church sees marriage when they stated in Faithful Citizenship that marriage "must be protected as a lifelong commitment between a man and a woman" (20).

This teaching sees the well-being of each individual and of society as closely tied to the health and stability of both marriage and family life.

For this reason the church often stresses the need for society to have a proper understanding of the nature of marriage and to do all that is needed to protect this institution as well as the family itself.

Beyond the definition of marriage, the bishops' statement said that public policies—such as those related to employment, taxes, divorce, and welfare—should aim "to help families stay together and to reward responsibility and sacrifice for children" (20).

Economics

Much is said and written these days about protecting the family. That discussion tends to focus upon threats to family life that are present in contemporary culture. Such threats are seen in efforts to redefine marriage. They are found as well in the media's presentation of family life and values. Catholic teaching shares this concern as it cautions against the unregulated development of television and the internet, and the increase in materials condoning violence and pornography.

Catholic social teaching reminds us of another threat confronting families, this one related to economics. "Because financial and economic factors have such an impact on the well-being and stability of families, it is important that just wages be paid to those who work to support their families and that generous efforts be made to aid poor families" (Faithful Citizenship, 20). This statement reflects what the social sciences have recognized for a very long time. Financial or economic stress has a great potential for disrupting healthy family living. The earliest social encyclicals emphasized the need for workers to receive adequate wages so that they would be able to support their families (On the Condition of Labor, 35).

More contemporary Catholic teaching urges that all economic and social policies, especially those related to work, should be evaluated from the perspective of how they impact the strength and stability of family life. "Efficiency and competition in the marketplace must be moderated by greater concern for the way work schedules and compensation support or threaten the bonds between spouses and between parents and children" (Economic Justice for All, 93). Adequate income and reasonable work schedules and conditions provide the possibility, at least, that workers might give some attention to the needs of others. It is unlikely that Aaron would be involved in either charity or justice actions if his own employment did not provide sufficient income.

Education

Another topic commonly found in discussions about families is that of education. Catholic social teaching offers a number of perspectives on education, some of them quite familiar to most of us, others less so. The starting point for this teaching is that every person has a right to a quality education—not just those living in more affluent societies, and not just males. Pope John XXIII added that for certain people higher education should be a possibility. "Every effort should be made to ensure that persons be enabled, on the basis of merit, to go on to higher studies, so that, as far as possible, they may occupy posts and take on responsibilities in human society in accordance with their natural gifts and the skills they have acquired" (Peace on Earth, 13). All education, including vocational training and college, represent a way of developing the talents God has given us and placing those gifts at the service of the larger society.

At the primary and secondary level, education is regarded as a fundamental parental responsibility with the educational systems standing in support of these parental efforts. Because of this responsibility parents should be able to choose the educational system or school best suited to the needs of their children. Open enrollment, vouchers, and other means might be considered to provide choices for parents, though care must be taken to ensure these parental choices are equally available to families with limited income (Faithful Citizenship, 20). Underlying all of this is the need for adequate funding to educate everyone whether they are in public, private, or religious schools.

The social teachings present challenges to our normal understanding of the kind of education that should be provided to younger members of families. Faithful Citizenship articulates one: "We must ensure that our nation's young people—especially the poor, those with disabilities, and the most vulnerable—are properly prepared to be good citizens, to lead productive lives, and to be socially and morally responsible in the complicated and technologically challenging world of the twenty-first century" (24).

Education is about more than preparing to make a living as adult members of society. It is about that, to be sure; but it is more. Economic Justice for All captures this rich sense of the purpose of education when speaking about the church's own role in this effort.

> Since the Christian vocation is a call to transform oneself and society with God's help, the educational efforts of the Church must encompass the twin purposes of personal sanctification and social reform in the light of Christian values. (341)

All education can contribute to the complete development of each person in such a way as to facilitate this personal growth and transformation. It leads us to recognize that our ongoing conversion changes our relationship with our neighbors and makes us responsible for the societies in which we live. Aaron's volunteer work and justice advocacy provide an example of such ownership and accountability.

Catholic social teaching calls for an education to justice that awakens within all of us a critical sense to be able to reflect on our society and its values, and to be able "to renounce these values when they cease to promote justice in all men" (Justice in the World, 51). Education for justice is a necessary part of everyone's education and formation. This education aims to have consciences recognize what is happening in the world and the values behind these developments. This education seeks improvements in society and, ultimately, the transformation of the world. The church itself must attend to these aspects of education.

> For these reasons the Church must incorporate into all levels of her educational system the teaching of social justice and the biblical and ethical principles that support it. We call on our universities, in particular, to make Catholic social teaching, and the social encyclicals of the popes a part of their curriculum, especially for those whose vocation will call them to an active role in U.S. economic and political decision-making. (Economic Justice for All, 342)

Participation

One of the more interesting developments in Catholic social teaching is the emergence of the principle of participation. The earliest expressions of this teaching appear in Pope Leo XIII's recognition of the right of workers to form associations (unions) to protect their interests. John XXIII took this a step further when he advocated that workers should be given a voice in the management of the workplace and even in its ownership. These early positions regarding workers would gradually develop into a recognition of the right of participation for all people in every area of life.

Right and duty

All human beings have a duty to take part in the great challenge of building the common good, and a right to be involved in decision making processes that affect their lives. To be involved, to participate, is one of

the growing desires of modern persons. In his Call to Action in 1971
Pope Paul VI recognized this desire.

> While scientific and technological progress continues to overturn
> man's surroundings, his patterns of knowledge, work, consumption,
> and relationships, two aspirations persistently make themselves felt
> in these new contexts, and they grow stronger to the extent that he
> becomes better informed and better educated: the aspiration to
> equality and the aspiration to participation, two forms of man's
> dignity and freedom. (22)

Two points in this statement are especially noteworthy. The first is that
this growing desire for participation is at least partly the result of people
becoming educated. As people are "better informed and better educated"—in any country and in any walk of life—they seek to have a voice
in decisions that affect their lives. This goes hand in hand with Catholic
teaching on the right to education. Education promotes the growth and
development of the person and it nurtures within each of us a critical
awareness of what is happening in the world.

The second point to note in Paul VI's statement is that equality and
participation are "two forms of man's dignity and freedom." For persons
to realize their dignity and function with the necessary level of responsibility for themselves and others around them, they must be able to take
part in decision making. Pope John XXIII recognized this earlier when
discussing the needs of workers. Persons engaged in productive activity
have an innate need to assume greater responsibility. This is a characteristic of human nature. This is also one of the ways in which each of
us grows in our ability to utilize our God-given talents for our needs
and for the well-being of our communities. It is how we realize human
dignity (Christianity and Social Progress, 82). The U.S. Catholic bishops
summarize all of this in Economic Justice for All.

> Basic justice demands the establishment of minimum levels of
> participation in the life of the human community for all persons.
> The ultimate injustice is for a person or group to be treated actively
> or abandoned passively as if they were nonmembers of the human
> race. To treat people this way is effectively to say they simply do not
> count as human beings. (77)

A necessary part of our full human development is to have a voice, to
take part in shaping our immediate lives as well as the broad social

context within which we live those lives. This right and duty is to participate in the effort to build the common good and seek the well-being of all. Each of us according to our abilities is called to join in contributing to the progress of our own communities and, to the extent possible, to the shaping of the larger society. This right must be respected by public authorities. This duty must be carried out by each person (The Church in the Modern World, 65).

Social/economic/political

Continuing the development of this right to participate, the World Synod of Bishops in 1971 stressed that this right applies to all areas of organized social life—economic, social, and political (Justice in the World, 18). Earlier Catholic social documents gradually developed this theme in relation to the workplace, where workers should have a greater voice in decision making regarding the enterprise. This is a way for each worker to learn greater responsibility, not only for his workplace environment, but also for the larger society (Christianity and Social Progress, 97). The Second Vatican Council applied this right of participation to economic development on the national level, stressing that such efforts must remain under the people's control.

> It must not be left to the sole judgment of a few men or groups possessing excessive economic power, or of the political community alone, or of certain especially powerful nations [to determine the direction of economic development]. It is proper, on the contrary, that at every level the largest possible number of people have an active share in directing that development. (The Church in the Modern World, 65)

People have a right to be involved—directly or indirectly—in decision making processes that affect their lives. This right of participation applies to all areas of life. Western democratic societies tend to emphasize the right of political participation and consequently promote democratic forms of government. Catholic social teaching reminds us that this right is not limited to the political arena. It must take root as well in the field of economics and lead to broader sharing of economic power and to decisions that are more accountable to the common good (Economic Justice for All, 297).

Finally, this right of participation applies as well to the life of individual nations where each country has the right to determine its own development, including its form of government. Catholic social teaching tells us that the church does not advocate one style of governance over another. Each nation has the right to determine its own social, economic, and political structures without interference from any other nation, a point stated unambiguously in Justice in the World: "[A]ll peoples should be able to become the principal architects of their own economic and social development" (71). Each nation must choose its own course in promoting the common good. Ideally, that path will allow for the largest possible number of citizens to be involved in the governance process. The right of participation applies to all areas of life.

Discussion

1. To what extent does our society reflect or not reflect Catholic social teaching on the common good?

2. What is your understanding of the role of government? How does that understanding compare with Catholic teaching?

3. What do you consider the greatest threats to families?

4. What does this statement say to you: "People have a right to be involved in decision making processes that affect their lives"?

Actions

1. Carefully read a newspaper over the next week looking for an example of where someone's economic interests have come into conflict with the larger community.

2. Talk with someone whose volunteering efforts have led her to become more politically active. What motivates her? What challenges has she faced?

3. Check with your parish to see if any form of education for justice is happening. Can you identify any use of Catholic social teachings?

Chapter 4

Rights and Responsibilities

Joanne is grateful for the good health of her family members. She is also aware that one serious medical problem will bring a major financial setback. Joanne, along with her husband Bill and their three children, are among the forty-five million citizens of the United States without health insurance. Bill is a full-time chef whose restaurant offers no employee benefits. Joanne works for a local hospital which keeps her weekly hours just below the level at which benefits become mandatory. They keep their doctor and dental visits to a minimum, sometimes delaying a visit during illness, always fearful this may lead to more serious medical problems. Joanne and Bill are both hard workers and sometimes one will take a second job when finances are particularly tight. They do what they can to get by in a society that praises family values but doesn't regard such needs as health care, housing, and adequate employment as basic rights.

∰

A discussion of rights and responsibilities can go in many different directions. In the United States today there is much discussion about personal responsibility. Often that conversation represents an argument to reduce the level of government involvement in social services, leaving people like Joanne with little hope for some kind of health insurance coverage. At the same time we hear a lot about individual rights. Television commercials incessantly remind us of all the good things in life that we should have. People drive high fuel-consumption cars and trucks and noisy recreational vehicles with little concern for their impact on others in the community. The guiding norm seems to be: if I can afford it, I have a right to it.

These cultural factors add to the difficulty of understanding what Catholic social teaching has to say about rights and responsibilities. Two quick introductory points need to be made. First, Catholic teaching is at its best when it considers rights and responsibilities together. We cannot appreciate either except in relationship to the other. Each acts as a qualifier on the other. To speak only of rights—as happens so often in our society—is to ignore how these rights are limited by responsibilities to others. To focus only on personal responsibility risks overlooking or even denying the rights to which every person may lay claim.

A second point about rights and responsibilities in Catholic social teaching is that they exist within a social context. As humans live and grow within various forms of communities, so their rights and responsibilities take on meaning within this social environment as well. It is within community—within society—that we best appreciate the expectations that flow from human rights and human responsibilities.

Rights and Human Dignity

From a Catholic perspective any discussion of human rights begins with human dignity, the foundation of all rights. Every person enjoys a sacred dignity bestowed by the Creator. This dignity of human persons is grounded in the belief that all of us are created by God, redeemed by Christ, and called to communion with God. Within creation humans enjoy a special relationship with God. Made in God's image, our life's vocation is to respond to God's call.

The dignity of the human person and the resultant sacredness of human life provide the foundation for the most basic of all human rights: the right to life. Catholic moral theology recognizes that each and every life is a gift from God. All of us are dependent upon God for our very existence. From that perspective the right to life is a qualified right in the sense that no one has a right to life beyond what the Creator may have intended. At the same time the affirmation of the sacredness of human life and the right to life that every human enjoys is a claim directed towards every other human being. This claim asserts that no one may end the life of another human person except to defend one's own life and the lives for whom one is responsible. Catholic social teaching claims that everyone has the fundamental right to life.

The right to life means more than the right to be born. In Catholic teaching this right begins at conception and ends at natural death. Central to this teaching is the claim that every person also has a right to those conditions necessary for living a decent life. Faithful Citizenship summarizes these rights as "faith and family life, food and shelter, education and employment, health care and housing" (14). It is never enough to defend a person's right to be born without also supporting whatever is needed to live that life with dignity. Peace on Earth in 1961 became the first social encyclical to discuss in great detail the right to life's basic necessities.

> Beginning our discussion of the rights of man, we see that every man has the right to life, to bodily integrity, and to the means which are suitable for the proper development of life; these are primarily food, clothing, shelter, rest, medical care, and finally the necessary social services. Therefore a human being also has the right to security in cases of sickness, inability to work, widowhood, old age, unemployment, or in any other case in which he is deprived of the means of subsistence through no fault of his own. (11)

Catholic social teaching regards these human rights as essential for the safeguarding of human dignity. To deny a person any one of these rights (such as food, shelter, or health care) is to make it more difficult for such a person to realize her dignity and to be as fully responsible for herself and others as she is called to be. Joanne and Bill are doing everything they can to be good parents and good citizens. Their lack of health insurance, and the potentially serious problem this represents, endangers the long-term health of their family members as well as their ability to contribute to the larger community, all a way of realizing human dignity. Catholic teaching sees these fundamental rights as "the minimum conditions for life in community" (Economic Justice for All, 17). The teaching also notes that these rights are universal. A person living in Asia, Africa, or Latin America has the same right to these basic necessities of life as does someone living in the United States. Whether these rights are protected in any society becomes a primary criterion for evaluating the just workings of that society's institutions.

In recent decades Catholic social teaching has introduced two new accents into the discussion of human rights that relate to the protection of human dignity. In the United States the Catholic bishops speak of economic and social rights in the same conversation as civil and political rights (Economic Justice for All, 80). It is not enough to grant people the right to vote or to be free of discrimination. The protection of human rights includes insuring all citizens the right to employment or income so they may obtain the goods essential for a dignified life such as food, health care, or housing. The bishops note the parallels between today's economic challenges and the political challenge faced by the founders of this nation:

> In order to create a new form of political democracy they were compelled to develop ways of thinking and political institutions that had never existed before. Their efforts were arduous and their goals imperfectly realized, but they launched an experiment in the protection of civil and political rights that has prospered through the efforts of those who came after them. *We believe the time has come for a similar experiment in securing economic rights: the creation of an order that guarantees the minimum conditions of human dignity in the economic sphere for every person.* (95)

A second emphasis in more recent social documents is that placed on the right of participation. As noted in the previous chapter, everyone has the right to participate in decision-making processes that affect their lives. Increasingly this right to participate is recognized as the guarantor of many other rights.

Rights and Healthy Communities

This Catholic support of human rights should not be confused with a Western cultural reverence for individual rights outside a framework of social responsibility. While Catholic teaching does promote personal rights, it balances these rights with mutual responsibilities and a concern for the well-being of the larger society. For this reason human rights are seen as the foundation of social harmony as well as international peace. We cannot have healthy communities and a peaceful society if human dignity is not respected and rights are not protected. The strife and turmoil that results from the abuse of human rights contradict any notion of harmonious relationships either within nations or across borders. Pope Paul VI warned of this connection between denial of rights and social unrest when he wrote how the poor were becoming aware of their undeserved hardship: "the temptation becomes stronger to risk being swept away toward types of messianism which give promises but create illusions. The resulting dangers are patent: violent popular reactions, agitation toward insurrection, and a drifting toward totalitarian ideologies" (On the Development of Peoples, 11).

John XXIII had stated this point in more positive language when he pointed out that maintaining personal rights and duties is the principal way of guaranteeing the common good. Heads of state, then, and all civil authorities must endeavor to respect, protect, and coordinate these rights. In this way it is possible for everyone in society not simply to claim their rights, but to balance the exercise of their rights against the needs of the broader community. In this way each person carries out his or her duties and makes the necessary contribution to the common good (Peace on Earth, 60).

Protecting human rights is necessary for the integral development of every person within society. No one can easily grow in moral responsibility, direct their lives, and contribute to society if they must worry about whether they will eat today or where they might be sleeping tonight. One's living conditions must allow a person to become conscious of his dignity and to exercise the needed freedom and responsibility of a person made in the image and likeness of God (The Church in the Modern World, 31). These fundamental personal rights—civil, political, social, and economic—are necessary for human dignity.

Respect for these rights contributes to the development of both individuals and society. Denial of any one of these rights, such as health care or education or participation, harms not only the individuals directly affected, but the larger community as a whole, causing tensions and divisions and weakening the solidarity among citizens (Economic Justice for All, 80). Denial of such rights also may result in practical, costly consequences to society. Joanne and Bill sometimes delay seeking medical help for themselves or one of their children because they can't afford a visit to the doctor. This delay may lead to more costly medical procedures that the city or county will have to pay for in the future.

There is an important relationship between respecting individual rights and building healthy communities. We see this also in the church's teaching on intermediate associations, those many voluntary groups and organizations that stand between individuals and the government. Every person has a right to belong to such organizations of their choice—churches, book clubs, organized charities. By exercising our right to join such groups we contribute something to the community as a whole. Catholic social teaching first developed this connection between the exercise of individual rights and the building of community in its writings on workers' rights to join unions and participate in decision making within the enterprise. This kind of association and participation becomes a training ground for responsible involvement in the larger society. For this reason Economic Justice for All reminds us that labor unions and other intermediate organizations "are an indispensable element of social life" (104).

A basic Catholic teaching on human rights is that they cannot be denied or taken away. These rights come with being human, granted by God, unable to be extinguished by other humans. This is the meaning of John XXIII's assertion: "Indeed, precisely because one is a person one has rights and obligations flowing directly and simultaneously from one's very nature. And as these rights and obligations are universal and inviolable, so they cannot in any way be surrendered" (Peace on Earth, 9). This is part of the rationale behind the church's opposition to the death penalty. Regardless of what a person has done and in spite of having committed a terrible crime against other humans, a criminal never relinquishes his God-given sacred dignity and right to life. The only justifiable reason for using the death penalty against such a person would be to protect citizens, something which today can be accomplished short of the death penalty.

Finally, in the interplay between personal rights and building healthy communities there is a place for persons to decide not to exercise certain personal rights because of the needs of the larger society. An example might be a person choosing not to purchase a vehicle with poor gas mileage because society needs to conserve energy. This is a way of contributing to the common good. It is also recognizing the possibility of rights being in conflict. Paul VI had this in mind when he used the now famous phrase "preferential respect due the poor." "The more fortunate should renounce some of their rights so as to place their goods more generously at the service of others" (A Call to Action, 23).

Responsibilities

A discussion of human rights is incomplete if it does not address responsibilities. The realization of human dignity is not possible if we focus only upon the claims each of us can make upon one another and upon society. A Catholic understanding of human dignity includes the central notion that persons are responsible for the direction of their lives.

Each of us has the ability and duty to direct our lives towards the end intended by the Creator. While that end may not always be clear to us, we are able to recognize good choices in our lives—choices that are good for us, good for our neighbors, and good for the larger society. Human dignity requires that each of us has what we need to live a reasonably decent life. Human dignity also requires each of us to take responsibility for our lives, for the well-being of our neighbors, and for the common good.

Build community

This balance between rights and responsibilities is necessary for the proper development of individual persons and of society.

> Those, therefore, who claim their own rights, yet altogether forget or neglect to carry out their respective duties, are people who build with one hand and destroy with the other. Since men are social by nature they are meant to live with others and to work for one another's welfare. (Peace on Earth, 30–31)

One of our greatest responsibilities is to help build healthy communities—local, state, and national. That effort is made difficult if we are overly concerned about our own rights. Certainly, we must attend to what we need for our own growth as morally responsible persons. Daily physical, material needs are part of that. John XXIII reminded us of this when he wrote that "he who possesses certain rights has likewise the duty to claim those rights as marks of his dignity" (Peace on Earth, 44). Nonetheless, one of our more serious responsibilities is to balance the claims we make—even rightful claims—with the needs of the broader community. Those needs include respecting the rights of others. They also include foregoing some things to which we may have a rightful claim but which may detract from the strength and well-being of society.

Defending rights

One final consideration of our responsibilities is in the area of defending specific rights that come under attack. In addition to looking out for the well-being and healthy development of society, we also have a duty to stand up in defense of human rights. This may take the form of speaking up for the right of immigrants to receive social services in our state or county. It may involve standing with minorities experiencing discrimination in a local university. This defense of specific human rights can be an effective witness to what Catholic social teaching says about human dignity, rights, and responsibilities. This teaching warns that it is not enough to respect dignity and rights in the abstract. That respect is of little value if it does not find expression in the practical world of daily living. We must not only respect human rights, but secure and defend them (Faithful Citizenship, 14). Again, the social document that launched the church's modern discussion of human rights underscores this point. "It is not enough, for example, to acknowledge and respect every man's right to the means of subsistence if we do not strive to the best of our ability for a sufficient supply of what is necessary for his sustenance" (Peace on Earth, 32).

Rights Under Threat

In our world today the opportunity to defend human rights and dignity is always present. It is difficult to imagine a time in history when there were more unnecessary and avoidable threats against that part of creation made in the image and likeness of God.

Life

None of these threats is more serious than the direct attacks against human life discussed in chapter 2. Abortion, euthanasia, capital punishment—these actions among others represent the most dramatic and direct threats to human rights and dignity because their aim is to end life. Even as the number of abortions in the United States is declining, the use of embryonic stem cell research is gaining support. The foreseeable future appears unlikely to be free of the different direct attacks against human life. Clear as that may be, these acts are not the only ways in which the dignity of the human person comes under attack. Along with the threat to life itself, we see many ways in which the possibility of living that life with dignity is threatened. These threats take different shape in different parts of the world, but all of them share one common effect. They diminish the chances of people to live their life to the fullest and to realize the sacred dignity their Creator has given them.

Life's supports

Globally one of the greatest threats to people living a dignified life is the lack of safe and nutritious *food*. In the developed world new technologies for producing ever greater quantities of food are constantly emerging. In spite of this the human family faces record numbers of people malnourished, chronically hungry, and even starving. The Food and Agricultural Organization reported in 2004 that an estimated 852 million people were undernourished (Faithful Citizenship, 29). Each year more than five million children die of hunger and related causes. Even in the United States, and in spite of its affluence, almost four million households suffered from hunger in 2003 (Food Research Action Coalition, 2005).

These are the tragic circumstances that prompt Catholic social teaching to remind us that

> a man can scarcely arrive at the needed sense of responsibility unless his living conditions allow him to become conscious of his dignity, and to rise to his destiny by spending himself for God and for others. (The Church in the Modern World, 31)

Food is one of the most fundamental of human rights, and one of the most unrealized. The denial of this right on such a massive scale prevents millions of people from responding to God's call to develop and utilize their gifts in the service of God's people.

Threats to human rights, to those things needed to live a dignified life, appear in other forms here in the United States and throughout the world. The problem of *homelessness* is not diminishing. It is estimated there are approximately 3.5 million homeless persons in this country at any time (National Coalition for the Homeless, 2002). People are homeless for a variety of reasons including mental illness and addictions. Tragically, many other homeless persons find themselves without shelter because they simply cannot afford the housing available, rental or otherwise. Catholic social teaching always has regarded adequate shelter as necessary for leading a truly human life (The Church in the Modern World, 26). The Catholic bishops have termed the lack of safe, affordable housing in the United States "a national crisis" (Faithful Citizenship, 23).

This crisis expresses itself in many forms. Young adults of middle income families find it difficult to buy their first home. Politicians and church-based community organizing efforts tend to respond quickly to this dimension of the housing crisis. There are other expressions of this crisis that receive far less attention—individuals who live on the streets, families who sleep in a car, women in transition from addiction recovery programs without the means to secure housing in any form. These are the expressions of homelessness to which the preferential option for the poor says we must respond.

Still another threat to human dignity in the United States appears in the area of *health care*. The church has always recognized that decent health care—along with food and housing—should be available to all. This is a moral imperative for the protection of human dignity. In 2003 forty-five million Americans were without health insurance coverage, placing their access to needed medical services in jeopardy. Faithful Citizenship summarizes Catholic social teaching on this topic.

> Affordable and accessible health care is an essential safeguard of human life, a fundamental human right, and an urgent national priority. We need to reform the nation's health care system, and this reform must be rooted in values that respect human dignity, protect human life, and meet the needs of the poor and uninsured. (23)

Joanne and Bill are just one example of millions of working American families whose well-being is daily compromised by our society's unwillingness to provide this human right, to provide some form of health insurance for every citizen.

In the area of *labor* we see two particular rights that are under increasing threat in the United States today. One is the denial of just compensation for labor. Millions of U.S. citizens today work full time yet remain below the poverty level because their wages are inadequate. A second threat to workers today relates to their right to organize, to form unions. Beginning with Pope Leo XIII's first social encyclical, On the Condition of Labor (1891), the church has repeatedly voiced its support for collective bargaining among workers. To deny this right is an attack upon human dignity itself. Yet in 1985 the U.S. Catholic bishops felt the need to restate their opposition to ongoing efforts to destroy existing unions and to prevent workers from organizing new ones (Economic Justice for All, 104).

There is one final area in which we see threats to basic human rights necessary for respecting human dignity. That is the area of *immigration*. The gospel calls us to love our neighbor and welcome the stranger, especially the neighbor who seeks a decent life by emigrating from her native country. This is a right long recognized in Catholic social teaching.

> Every human being has the right to freedom of movement and of residence within the confines of his own country; and, when there are just reasons for it, the right to emigrate to other countries and take up residence there. (Peace on Earth, 25)

Today nations experience a heightened concern regarding terrorism, a phenomenon that leads to more restrictive immigration policies. Clearly nations have a right to promote their own security. Likewise, sovereign states have the right to control their borders, but this is not an absolute right. Already in 1952 Pope Pius XII wrote that authorities must seek a balance between the legitimate concerns of more affluent nations and the needs of immigrants (On the Spiritual Care to Migrants). More recently a joint pastoral letter from the Catholic bishops of Mexico and the United States reminds us that the right to immigrate is grounded in the principle that the goods of creation are meant to satisfy the needs of all peoples.

> The Church recognizes that all the goods of the earth belong to all people. When persons cannot find employment in their country of origin to support themselves and their families, they have a right to find work elsewhere in order to survive. Sovereign nations should provide ways to accommodate this right. (Strangers No Longer, 35)

Christians, as individuals and as local churches, must welcome immigrants and defend their right to basic necessities for a dignified life. These include livable wages, decent housing, health care, and education. In their pastoral statement, Welcoming the Stranger Among Us (2000), the U.S. Catholic bishops emphasize that all immigrants have a right to respectable living conditions, regardless of their legal status (11). In recent years various rights of immigrants have come under threat from new immigration legislation (1996) and from efforts in different states to restrict immigrant access to tax-supported education and health care.

A final point on this topic is to note that the most effective way to reduce immigration into any country is by addressing the causes that lead people to leave their own lands—by addressing "the political, social, and economic inequities that contribute to it" (Faithful Citizenship, 24). Pope John Paul II elaborated on this in a 2004 World Day of Migrants and Refugees statement when he stated that building conditions of peace must include protecting the right to live in peace and dignity in one's own country.

> . . . it is possible for every country to guarantee its own population, in addition to freedom of expression and movement, the possibility to satisfy basic needs such as food, health care, work, housing and education; the frustration of these needs forces many into a position where their only option is to emigrate. (3)

We must support the needs and rights of immigrants in our country, especially those who choose to live in our local communities. At the same time we need to advocate for just economic and political relations between nations, for trade relations favorable to developing nations, and for generosity on the part of wealthy nations in foreign assistance. All of this addresses the basic needs of people before they decide to emigrate from their native lands. All of this respects the right of every person anywhere on the globe to live in peace and dignity in one's own country.

Prioritizing rights

The right to life and the right to whatever is needed to live that life with dignity cover a lot of ground. This topic presents a complex and sometimes confusing picture of needs that must be addressed if human dignity is to be respected. Some people today draw a divide between the right to life and all other human rights (food, health care, housing, etc.). In their thinking, the right to life—and this often means the right to be born—is the most important of all rights and should receive more of our attention than other rights. There is a certain theoretical logic in this position: if you don't protect the right of a person to be born, why worry about meeting that person's need for food or health care? Confronting the abstract logic of this position are some very practical problems.

To prioritize rights in this manner is to make judgments about the relative value of human lives at different stages. The obvious questions follow. Is the life of an unborn person more valuable or more important than the life of a one-year-old child dying from starvation in the Sudan? Is that unborn life more valuable than that of a thirty-year-old woman in Detroit whose illness has reached a life-threatening stage because she did not have the money for medical treatment earlier when this disease could have been stopped? This is not to diminish the importance of the lives of the unborn, but to remind us that every human life is sacred, that every human life enjoys a dignity given by the Creator.

A further danger that comes with prioritizing rights in this way is the implied order of response. If the right to life of the unborn is the most important of human rights, then it would seem that our limited time, energy, and resources need to be directed toward the defense of those particular lives. The logical consequence of this position is that we don't allow other human needs (food, housing, health care) to distract us or consume resources until the struggle to defend the right to life of the unborn has been won. Neither our moral theology nor our intuitive instincts support that kind of thinking.

Catholic social teaching tells us that every human life is sacred—in every part of the world, at every age and stage of development. The life of the one in the womb is sacred not because he or she is an innocent unborn person, but because he or she is a person created in the image and likeness of God—the same as a twenty-year-old man struggling with AIDS or the homeless single mother of two who spends her nights in an emergency shelter. Prioritizing human rights risks overlooking the universal character of human dignity and the right of every human to be born and to live their life until natural death with their basic needs met.

We must defend all human rights because all of them are necessary for the full development of every person. We defend them as well because a healthy society and harmonious relations among nations depend upon respect for life at every stage of its development. As individuals we are called to stand up for persons or groups whose rights are threatened. Our own lives are vocational responses to God's call. Our effort to become whom we are called to be is not complete if we allow God's image to be degraded in fellow human beings. The 1971 document Justice in the World tells us that part of the Christian's response to Christ's saving act is in our deeds of justice (56). Earlier in the document we read of the necessary connection between faith and justice.

> Faith in Christ, the Son of God and the Redeemer, and love of neighbor constitute a fundamental theme of the writers of the New Testament. According to St. Paul, the whole of the Christian life is summed up in faith effecting that love and service of neighbor which involve the fulfillment of the demands of justice. (33)

The demands of justice require us to respond to any threat against the dignity and rights of human beings in our own nation or anywhere in the world. The opportunities for such responses are many. Our challenge is not to prioritize human rights but to recognize all of them as necessary, and to defend any right that comes under threat. Each of us has different gifts and skills to lend to that response. Each of us has different experiences and passions that will lead us to the defense of particular rights. The Spirit works through all of us, patiently.

Discussion

1. Catholic teaching places a great emphasis upon the dignity of the human person. What is the basis for this claim to human dignity?

2. Identify one human rights issue that has a particular appeal to you. How might you respond?

3. Explain how failure to respect and support any human right is harmful to the larger community, to society.

4. What connection does Catholic social teaching make between the right to be born and the right to health care or to food?

Action

1. Spend some time at a local food shelf or meals program. Do the people coming for food match the expectation you have of "hungry persons" in the area?

2. Visit a local agency that works on behalf of immigrants and ask people there what the main challenges are that immigrants face in your community.

3. Ask a local employer (discount retailer, hospital) about their benefits for employees. Do they provide health care? To all employees?

Chapter 5

Option for the Poor and Vulnerable

St. Joseph's Church has a long history of supporting charities—special collections, community food shelf, other service projects. Recently the parish started a Social Ministry Committee with the goals of promoting awareness of Catholic social teaching, providing more opportunities for parishioners to become involved in charity/service projects, and providing similar opportunities for parishioners to engage in social justice/change projects. As the committee became more familiar with Catholic social teaching, members felt a need to place more emphasis upon social justice. They hope to see their parish working for changes that might help people to move out of poverty, to be less dependent upon the charity of other persons. Today St. Joseph's Church complements its efforts to bring relief to persons in need—charity/service—with involvement in the more challenging, and sometimes controversial, actions in support of systemic change—social justice. These include working with the state Catholic Conference to promote legislation aimed at helping the poor, developing local markets for craft goods made by indigenous people of Central America, and advocating for the needs and rights of immigrants in the local community.

☙ℰ❧

As I write this chapter hundreds of thousands of pilgrims are streaming into the Vatican to view the body of Pope John Paul II. Few leaders in this era have won the love and respect of so many people around the world as has this pontiff. Undoubtedly there are many reasons for the worldwide popularity of this pope. One explanation is John Paul II's defense of human dignity and his untiring advocacy for the poor of this world. In his commitment to persons who are poor and vulnerable, John Paul II articulated one of the clearest messages in Catholic social teaching.

The theme of this chapter centers around one primary question: what is the Christian's responsibility to persons who are poor? The answer may seem quite simple, yet it has been developing in Catholic teaching for more than one hundred years. While there is obvious continuity in the church's teaching on this topic, there also is remarkable development. Other questions related to this theme include: How should the individual Christian respond to persons less well off? What do we mean by preferential option? What is the role of society in addressing poverty? How should the church as an institution respond? What about a parish like St. Joseph's?

Poverty

Poverty can take as many forms as one's definition of the term allows. The church's teaching always has recognized that alongside economic poverty we can speak of other ways in which persons are hindered from realizing the fullness of their dignity. Spiritual poverty is an example as is cultural poverty. Within Catholic social teaching, however, the concern and the emphasis is upon involuntary economic poverty. Even the definition of economic poverty varies widely from the relative poverty in the United States to the absolute poverty found in many developing nations. While acknowledging and respecting such differences, our discussion in this chapter focuses upon any form of unwanted economic poverty.

A growing tragedy

A conversation about the Christian's responsibility to the poor begins with a recognition of the extent of poverty in our world. For many decades the social teachings of the church have been calling our attention to this tragic reality. The Second Vatican Council noted the growing separation between wealth and poverty in the mid-twentieth century. "Never has the human race enjoyed such an abundance of wealth, resources and economic power. Yet a huge proportion of the world's citizens is still tormented by hunger and poverty, while countless numbers suffer from total illiteracy" (The Church in the Modern World, 4). In his first encyclical Pope John Paul II contrasted the consumer civilization awash in a surplus of goods with the remaining societies that suffer from hunger "with many people dying each day of starvation and malnutrition" (Redeemer of Man, 16).

Earlier Pope Paul VI spoke not only of the extent of poverty in the world but also of the fact that we know this poverty exists.

> Today no one can be ignorant any longer of the fact that in whole continents countless men and women are ravaged by hunger, countless numbers of children are undernourished, so that many of them die in infancy, while the physical growth and mental development of many others are retarded and as a result whole regions are condemned to the most depressing despondency. (On the Development of Peoples, 45)

There is a certain indictment in this statement. Church leaders often note that the more affluent people in the world seem blinded to the existence of poverty, prevented from seeing by their own wealth and consumerist lifestyles. Paul VI here states that no one today can deny their own awareness of the horrible poverty that affects millions of people throughout the world. We do know. If ever there was a legitimate veil of ignorance that shielded us from knowing and responding to such living conditions, that veil has long been lifted.

The existence of such poverty today is a twofold tragedy—first, because of its harmful effects upon the poor themselves, and second, because of its negative impact upon those of us who are not poor, those of us who know that "countless men and women are ravaged by hunger" but choose to look away. This is both the tragedy and the scandal of poverty. The scandal rises out of the fact that we turn away, we who claim to be followers of the one who said "as long as you did it for one of these the least of my sisters and brothers, you did it for me" (Matt 25:40).

The bishops of the United States reflected this sad note when writing about poverty—especially among children—in this country. "Today children are the largest single group among the poor. This tragic fact seriously threatens the nation's future. That so many people are poor in a nation as rich as ours is a social and moral scandal that we cannot ignore (Economic Justice for All, 16).

Past acceptance

Rejection of poverty has not always been articulated with clarity and force. Earlier teachings encouraged the poor to resign themselves to the unhappy state in which they found themselves. Even the first of the modern Catholic social encyclicals, On the Condition of Labor, reflects this thinking.

> To suffer and to endure, therefore, is the lot of humanity, let men try as they may, no strength and no artifice will ever succeed in banishing from human life the ills and troubles which beset it.
>
> There is nothing more useful than to look at the world as it really is—and at the same time look elsewhere for a remedy to its troubles. (14)

Later in the same document Pope Leo XIII writes that Jesus calls the poor blessed and that they should find solace in him. These thoughts, he states, should temper the pride of those who are well off, and bring encouragement to those afflicted with poverty. These thoughts should move the affluent to generosity, and the poor "to tranquil resignation" (20). Leo certainly was not condoning poverty, as is evident in his call for the more affluent to share their resources with the poor. Given the political situation in Europe during the second half of the nineteenth century—especially with the rise of socialism and its call for the workers and the poor to revolt—the pope was more inclined to counsel charity and patience as the proper response to poverty.

Seeds of violence

Leo's successors were better able to recognize the social evils that might result from poverty. Pope Paul VI is an example. In 1967 he wrote that wealthier nations must share their resources with their poorer counterparts. "Besides, the rich will be the first to benefit as a result. Otherwise, their continued greed will certainly call down upon them the judgment of God and the wrath of the poor, with consequences no one can foretell" (On the Development of Peoples, 49).

In these situations, "whose injustice cries to heaven," the poor and the destitute are tempted "to right these wrongs to human dignity" through recourse to violence (30). Paul VI was not accepting or in any way condoning violence. In that same discussion he warned that recourse to violence is likely to bring on new injustices and new disasters. His warning is simply a reminder that in desperation, when hope is lost, any group of people is likely to resort to extreme actions.

The ever-growing poverty throughout the world today is planting the seeds of violence. In October 2001, following the tragedy of 9/11, the Vatican observer at the United Nations reflected on this connection between poverty and violence:

> Though poverty is not itself the cause of terrorism, we cannot success-fully combat terrorism if we do not address the worsening disparities between the rich and poor. We must recognize that global disparity is fundamentally incompatible with global security. (Vatican Address)

According to Catholic social teaching, the world's response to terrorism must not center upon war against countries suspected of harboring those who commit acts of terrorism. The response should include a serious commitment to understand and address whatever causes persons to engage in desperate and violent acts. Absolute poverty is one of those causes.

Barrier to initiative and responsibility

The human community must strive to overcome poverty for many reasons. One is to avoid the social disruption, tension and instability that often results from degrading living conditions. That is not the primary motivation for Christian efforts against poverty. Poverty is wrong because it prevents the realization of human dignity. Poverty makes it difficult for persons to respond to God's call in their lives, difficult to take re-sponsibility for their lives, difficult to contribute to the building of healthy community. The Second Vatican Council expressed this position.

> Now a man can scarcely arrive at the needed sense of responsibility unless his living conditions allow him to become conscious of his dignity, and to rise to his destiny by spending himself for God and for others. But human freedom is often crippled when a man falls into extreme poverty, just as it withers when he indulges in too many of life's comforts and imprisons himself in a kind of splendid isola-tion. (The Church in the Modern World, 31)

This document further observes that because so many people live with-out the basic necessities of life, "they are deprived of almost all possibility of acting on their own initiative and responsibility" (63). Their living and working conditions deny many of the poor the possibility of acting with the freedom needed to take responsibility for their own lives and the communities of which they are a part.

Pope Paul VI saw this relationship between extreme poverty and the denial of human dignity in global terms, noting that "whole populations destitute of necessities live in a state of dependence barring them from all initiative and responsibility, and all opportunity to advance culturally and share in social and political life" (On the Development of Peoples, 30). The World Synod of Bishops repeated this theme in their 1971 document, Justice in the World: "These stifling oppressions constantly give rise to great numbers of 'marginal' persons, ill-fed, inhumanly housed, illiterate, and deprived of political power as well as of the suitable means of acquiring responsibility and moral dignity" (10).

Catholic moral theology teaches that each of us is responsible for responding to God's love. Each of us is responsible for using the gifts God has given us to grow and mature into the morally responsible person God calls us to be. Catholic social teaching on poverty does not deny this personal responsibility resting on every human being. These teachings emphasize, however, what intuition and common sense already reveal—hunger, homelessness, oppression, lack of health care, and joblessness make it difficult to live out this basic responsibility. Pope John Paul II summarizes this teaching: "there are others—many who have little or nothing—who do not succeed in realizing their basic human vocation because they are deprived of essential goods" (On Social Concern, 28).

Our contribution

Catholic teaching on poverty is not only about persons who suffer poverty, though that is the church's central concern on this topic. The teaching also is about those of us who contribute to poverty, sometimes unknowingly. Pope John Paul II warned that a consumer attitude uncontrolled by ethics is an abuse of freedom by those with resources, an abuse that limits the freedom of those who do not have enough (Redeemer of Man, 16). It is not always easy to grasp how present rates of consumption in affluent nations harm those who don't have what they need in developing countries. In promoting awareness of Catholic teaching, the Social Ministry Committee of St. Joseph's Church helps parishioners to see how our practical, daily lifestyles may contribute to this poverty in other parts of the world.

In his final social encyclical, John Paul II called on us to evaluate our attitudes towards the poor and to see them as brothers and sisters sharing in our own dreams and goals. He encouraged us to abandon any outlook that sees the poor as a burden trying to consume what others have produced.

> The poor ask for the right to share in enjoying material goods and to make good use of their capacity for work, thus creating a world that is more just and prosperous for all. The advancement of the poor constitutes a great opportunity for the moral, cultural and even economic growth of all humanity. (On the Hundredth Anniversary, 28)

This statement reminds us of Pope Paul VI's observation that the struggle against poverty and destitution is not enough. That struggle must be part of an effort to build a world in which every person can live a fully dignified, human life free of any form of servitude, "a world where freedom is not an empty word and where the poor man Lazarus can sit down at the same table with the rich man" (On the Development of Peoples, 47). To do this requires us to recognize that the marginalized of the world share our human dignity, that they too are created by God, redeemed by Christ and called to communion with God. Only then are we able to recognize the gifts that each person—poor or rich—brings to the task of building this earth.

Sharing/Giving

What should be a Christian's response to persons who are poor? Is it simply a matter of contributing money? How much is enough? These questions are not uncommon among people whose generous spirit prods them to help others in need. These questions appear as well in the earliest Catholic social documents.

Superfluous income

Pope Leo XIII addressed the questions in terms of what we should do with our excess income, wealth, or resources. He noted that no one can be expected to give from what is needed to satisfy our own necessities or the needs of our dependents. He even allowed that a person may hold onto what is reasonably required "to keep up becomingly his condition in life. . . . But when necessity has been supplied, and one's position fairly considered, it is a duty to give to the indigent out of that which is left over" (On the Condition of Labor, 19).

Leo XIII further stated that this duty to give to the poor out of our extras, out of our superfluous goods, is not a requirement of justice except when the need is extreme. Rather, this duty to share with the poor is an expectation of Christian charity, one that cannot be enforced by human law. His immediate successors repeated Leo's emphasis upon the duty we have in charity to share our "extras" with the less fortunate, as seen in Pius XI's 1931 encyclical, On Reconstructing the Social Order: "At the same time a man's superfluous income is not left entirely to his own discretion. We speak of that portion of his income which he does not need in order to live as becomes his station" (50).

Clearly these popes wanted to underscore the fundamental biblical theme that we must share our resources with persons and groups who are in need. Their emphasis, however, was upon those resources which we don't need—our superfluous income. No attempt was made in these early documents to define "superfluous income," leaving each person to declare what income and resources they needed. It was up to each individual to determine what was needed to live his or her life "becomingly."

The generosity exhibited in so many parishes, like St. Joseph's, reflects this early Catholic social teaching on sharing our resources. Most church members are quite willing to give to special collections, to contribute to the food shelf, even to volunteer some of their free time to one charity or another. This willingness to help others is an important expression of Christian love. It is a recognition of the connectedness among all God's people. It is a first step upon which a Social Ministry Committee can build. Commendable as this generosity may be, it is limited by an attitude of giving what we don't need, giving out of our extras, giving from our superfluous goods.

What is superfluous?

It was not until Pope John XXIII that we see some attempt to define or at least describe how we should determine what is superfluous. In a 1962 radio and television message, this pope offered a striking criterion for making that determination:

> The obligation of every man, the urgent obligation of the Christian man, is to reckon what is superfluous by the measure of the needs

of others, and to see to it that the administration and the distribution of created goods serves the common good. (Quoted in The Church in the Modern World, footnote 147)

Pope John XXIII reverses the reference point for determining how we should respond to the poor. Previously the primary consideration was the giver—what can I afford to give, what do I have left over after all my needs have been satisfied? With John XXIII the primary focus is upon the poor—what do they need? The needs of others determine what I can afford to share. Their need becomes the measure of what is superfluous in my own life.

This statement by John XXIII did not appear originally in a major encyclical but was quoted in its entirety by the Second Vatican Council. It is clear that Pope John's teaching set in motion a re-evaluation of how we should look at the Christian's obligation to share with persons who are in need. This radio and television message from September 11, 1962 sets the tone for the church's teaching on solidarity that would be developed thirty years later during the pontificate of Pope John Paul II.

Universal purpose

Focusing upon the needs of the recipient continued with the Second Vatican Council in its statement that everyone has a right to a share of earthly goods sufficient to meet their needs.

The Fathers and Doctors of the Church held this view, teaching that men are obliged to come to the relief of the poor, and to do so not merely out of their superfluous goods. (The Church in the Modern World, 69)

With this statement, the Council says it is not adequate to give out of our superfluous goods, however they are defined. We are to assist those in need not out of our extras but from our substance. This new emphasis in Catholic social teaching rests on an ancient Christian belief, namely, that "God intended the earth and all that it contains for the use of every human being and people" (69).

The universal purpose of the goods of creation now becomes the foundation stone in Catholic social teaching for addressing how a Christian should respond to the poor. The answer is quite simple. Your possessions are not your own. They belong to God and are intended to meet the needs of all humans. So whatever form of legal ownership society endorses, the Christian must recognize that his lawful possessions are not only his, but they also are a form of common property that should benefit others as well. In a dramatic expression of the contemporary urgency surrounding this belief the Council extends a warning: "Since there are so many people in this world afflicted with hunger, this sacred Council urges all, both individuals and governments, to remember the saying of the Fathers: 'Feed the man dying of hunger, because if you have not fed him you have killed him'" (69).

In this context the Council reminds us of the long-held teaching in Catholic moral theology, articulated especially in the *Summa Theologica* of St. Thomas Aquinas: "If a person is in extreme necessity, he has the right to take from the riches of others what he himself needs (The Church in the Modern World, 69). Aquinas' discussion of this point further notes that such an action is not stealing because in extreme necessity all goods are common—God intended the goods of creation to meet the needs of everyone. Far beyond satisfying my personal needs and wants, these goods serve a universal purpose.

No right to keep for ourselves

Pope Paul VI summarized this teaching on how we should respond to the poor with his discussion about global poverty in the 1967 encyclical, On the Development of Peoples.

> It is well-known how strong were the words used by the Fathers of the Church to describe the proper attitude of persons who possess anything towards persons in need. To quote St. Ambrose: "You are not making a gift of your possessions to the poor person. You are handing over to him what is his. For what has been given in common for the use of all, you have arrogated to yourself. The world is given to all, and not only to the rich." (23)

Looking upon our possessions as common property to be shared with others is a theme present throughout the history of Catholic social teaching. Even Leo XIII's teaching on giving out of our superfluous goods is grounded in Aquinas' discussion of ownership and sharing.

> But if the question be asked, How must one's possessions be used? The Church replies without hesitation in the words of the same holy

doctor: "Man should not consider his outward possessions as his own, but as common to all, so as to share them without difficulty when others are in need." (On the Condition of Labor, 19)

The all-encompassing nature of this teaching is reflected in Pope John Paul II's encyclical, On Social Concern: "Those who are more influential because they have a greater share of goods and common services should feel responsible for the weaker and be ready to share with them all they possess" (39).

No document presents this teaching with the force and unnerving clarity as On the Development of Peoples. Reflecting on the poverty and suffering throughout the world, Pope Paul VI challenges any notion of ownership that exaggerates the owner's claim to hold on to what he possesses:

> [P]rivate property does not constitute for anyone an absolute and unconditional right. No one is justified in keeping for his exclusive use what he does not need, when others lack necessities. (23)

In the First Letter of John we see the question: "If someone who has the riches of this world sees his brother in need and closes his heart to him, how does the love of God abide in him?" (3:16). Our love of God must be reflected in our love of our neighbor, especially those most in need. If we are not able to share what we have with persons in need, we must question the quality of our relationship with God and our faithfulness to the demands of that relationship. That is the admonishment from the Scriptures, the early Christian writers, and Catholic social teaching. As Pope John Paul II stated in On the Hundredth Anniversary, responding to the needs of the poor provides "a great opportunity for the moral, cultural and even economic growth of all humanity" (28).

Preferential Option

The church's teaching regarding the Christian's response to the poor has developed noticeably since Pope Leo XIII gave us the first of the modern social encyclicals. None of these developments is as significant as the "option for the poor." Throughout the 1960s liberation theologians of Latin America were writing about the preferential option for the poor that should characterize Christian living. This included choosing to be in solidarity with the poor and committing oneself to working for changes to benefit the poor, changes in personal lifestyle, and in social, economic, and political structures.

Structural change to benefit the poor

Pope Paul VI in 1967 was suggesting that the Christian's response to the poor must go beyond contributing money and volunteering time. It also involves changing social and economic systems as well as public policies in ways that will benefit persons and nations in need. In his encyclical On the Development of Peoples, Paul VI challenges the rich and those who are relatively well off.

> Is he prepared to support out of his own pocket works and under-takings organized in favor of the most destitute? Is he ready to pay higher taxes so that the public authorities can intensify their efforts in favor of development? Is he ready to pay a higher price for im-ported goods so that the producer may be more justly rewarded? Or to leave this country, if necessary, and if he is young, in order to assist in this development of the young nations? (47)

Four years later, in his apostolic letter, A Call to Action, Paul VI em-ployed "option for the poor" language to describe how the Christian should respond to needs locally and globally.

> In teaching us charity, the Gospel instructs us in the preferential re-spect due to the poor and the special situation they have in society; the more fortunate should renounce some of their rights so as to place their goods more generously at the service of others. (23)

This preferential option for the poor calls us to respond to their needs in a far deeper manner than giving money, whether from our superflu-ous goods or from our substance. The option for the poor means more than sharing our personal resources with the needy. It means working for changes in our society and in the world, changes aimed at helping the less fortunate to live decent lives and to realize their dignity. This calls for changes in our personal lifestyle. It also calls us to support sys-temic, structural changes, especially in the economic and political arenas. It means supporting those changes in laws, public policies, and programs that are of primary benefit to those who are most in need. To make an option for the poor requires us to stand in solidarity with the poor. Only then are we able to see what needs to change in our own lives and in the structures of society.

How this might work is suggested by the U.S. Catholic bishops in their 1986 pastoral letter, Economic Justice for All. Our decisions regarding such issues as minimum wage or social security or health care should be judged by how these changes affect persons who are least well off. The basic moral criterion for all policy decisions and for the shaping of economic institutions nationally and globally is that these decisions and choices are at the service of everyone, but especially the poor (24). The bishops add that we must make a fundamental option for the poor as individuals and as a nation.

> The obligation to evaluate social and economic activity from the viewpoint of the poor and the powerless arises from the radical command to love one's neighbor as one's self. Those who are marginalized and whose rights are denied have privileged claims if society is to provide justice for all. (87)

Global implications

The global implications of this option for the poor are evident in the words of the bishops of the United States. Such implications are even more strongly recognized in the universal social teachings of the Vatican. Pope Paul VI had acknowledged that each nation naturally is the first to benefit from the gifts that God has bestowed on it and from the fruit of the labor of its people. Nonetheless, this provides no nation with a reason to keep its wealth for itself (On the Development of Peoples, 48). Not surprisingly, this statement comes from the pope who relied extensively on the early Christian principle regarding the universal purpose of the goods of creation.

Pope John Paul II also discussed this option or "love of preference" for the poor in global terms. "Today, furthermore, given the worldwide dimension which the social question has assumed, this love of preference for the poor, and the decisions which it inspires in us, cannot but embrace the immense multitudes of the hungry, the needy, the homeless, those without medical care and, above all, those without hope of a better future" (On Social Concern, 42).

John Paul II spoke of this option for the poor in the language of human dignity, highlighting what he referred to as the "human potential for the poor." His comments in On the Hundredth Anniversary remind one of the U.S. bishops' discussion of social justice in Economic Justice for All. The poor everywhere should be helped to improve their condition through work and to make their own contribution to the economic well-being of their respective societies. This cannot happen unless those who are poor—individuals and nations—are offered realistic opportunities.

> Creating such conditions calls for a concerted worldwide effort to promote development, an effort which also involves sacrificing the positions of income and of power enjoyed by the more developed economies. (52)

The preferential option for the poor cannot be realized without sacrifice on the part of those who are well off. Paul VI spoke of renouncing some of our rights so that we are in a better position to share our resources. John Paul II refers more globally to sacrificing positions of income and power.

Challenges

The option for the poor is a challenging and difficult aspect of Catholic social teaching. It does not allow us to rest comfortably in the knowledge that we have contributed money, perhaps a significant amount, to one or another charity on behalf of the poor. This teaching reminds us that charity is not enough. Rather, we must be willing to change our own lifestyles, and to change institutions, policies, and laws—all of this so that the poor may be less dependent upon our charity.

This teaching on the preferential option is difficult also because it names one group of people as deserving of special attention, namely, the poor. In a society that places strong emphasis upon equality before the law, this preferential consideration is easily discomforting. Catholic social teaching responds to this concern from several perspectives. The option for the poor is not an exclusive option, one that would lead us to ignore persons with other needs. Nor should it set one group against another. John Paul II encourages us to not allow this preferential option for the poor to exclude other groups. "This option is not limited to material poverty, since it is well known that there are many other forms of poverty, especially in modern society—not only economic but cultural and spiritual poverty as well" (On the Hundredth Anniversary, 57).

The church's teachings consistently have held that the justice and health of any society can be measured by how that society cares for its weakest members. Thus, by assisting the most vulnerable we are in fact strengthening the whole community. Economic Justice for All captures this point.

> The primary purpose of this special commitment to the poor is to enable them to become active participants in the life of society. It is to enable all persons to share in and contribute to the common good. The "option for the poor," therefore, is not an adversarial slogan that pits one group or class against another. Rather it states that the deprivation and powerlessness of the poor wounds the whole community. (88)

The suffering of the poor tells us how far we are from being a just society and, on a global level, from being a true human community. For our own health as a society, and as a family of nations, the tragedy of poverty must receive priority consideration. In the Catholic tradition we show a preferential option for the poor not only because it is good for us as a community, but also because we believe it is what Christ asks us to do: "As long as you did it for one of these the least of my sisters and brothers, you did it for me" (Matt 25:40). "As followers of Christ, we are challenged to make a fundamental 'option for the poor'—to speak for the voiceless, to defend the defenseless, to assess life styles, policies, and social institutions in terms of their impact on the poor" (Economic Justice for All, Introduction, 16).

Responding to Poverty

Responding to the needs of the poor is not the sole responsibility of individual Christians. Catholic social teaching always has recognized that one of the primary responsibilities of government is to look after the interests of the poor (On the Condition of Labor, 26). As noted earlier, how a society responds to its most vulnerable citizens—through its institutions and public policies—is the test of its justice or injustice. In the United States today more than thirty million people live in poverty, a particularly scandalous reality in a society with the resources that this nation enjoys. The bishops of this country consistently have called for more attention to this tragic reality as they did in 1986.

> The norms of human dignity and the preferential option for the poor compel us to confront this issue with a sense of urgency. Dealing

with poverty is not a luxury to which our nation can attend when it finds time and resources. Rather, it is a moral imperative of the highest priority. (Economic Justice for All, 170)

The church also carries a special responsibility towards the poor, what Pope John Paul II called an evangelical duty to stand beside the poor. The Social Ministry Committee at St. Joseph's Church—or in any parish—has no greater challenge than to articulate this message in words and actions that draw parishioners into this ministry. To stand beside the poor in charity and justice (service and change) means that we are willing to support changes that are of particular benefit to the poor and the marginalized. This is to engage in actions on behalf of justice and to make a preferential option for the poor. It is to live under the words—both comforting and condemning—from the Parable of the Last Judgment found in Matthew 25:40. The 1971 World Synod of Bishops also spoke of the "Church's vocation to be present in the heart of the world by proclaiming the Good News to the poor, freedom to the oppressed, and joy to the afflicted" (Justice in the World, 5).

If the church is to proclaim the gospel to the poor then it must be sure that its own lifestyle does not cloud this witness to the gospel. When the church is seen to be among the rich and the powerful, the credibility of its proclamation surely will be compromised. "In regard to temporal possessions, whatever be their use, it must never happen that the evangelical witness which the Church is required to give becomes ambiguous. The preservation of certain positions of privilege must constantly be submitted to the test of this principle" (47).

This lifestyle witness to the gospel is not only an expectation of bishops, priests and religious. It is a challenge to the laity as well. The lifestyle of everyone becomes material for an examination of conscience. Do we seek to live sparingly, with a deliberate effort to control our consumption, in ways that allow others with greater needs to live a life of dignity? Or, as the Synod asks, does belonging to the church place us "on a rich island within an ambient of poverty" (48)?

Discussion

1. What forms of economic poverty exist in your community?

2. On a global scale Catholic social teaching draws a connection between poverty and violence such as that seen in some acts of terrorism. Why does this teaching make this connection?

3. The option for the poor calls for changes on many levels. What are these changes?

4. What is the Christian's responsibility to persons who are economically poor?

Actions

1. Visit a social service agency (county, Catholic Charities, Lutheran Social Services) and ask someone there to give you the top three causes of poverty in the area.

2. Do an inventory to identify what charity and service projects your parish supports. Do the same to determine what justice and social change projects receive parish support.

3. Identify something in your lifestyle that you could change in order to benefit persons who are poor.

Chapter 6

The Dignity of Work and the Rights of Workers

Arturo rises at four o'clock every morning to begin milking cows. He and three other immigrants walk the short distance from their small trailer house to the large modern milking parlor where nearly a thousand Holsteins wait to be milked. Arturo and his friends are part of a new development in the rural Midwest. As moderate-sized family farms give way to large-scale livestock facilities, more employees are needed to do the work. Often these new workers are recently arrived immigrants hoping to make enough money to support themselves and send some to their families in Mexico. Arturo's wages are poverty level; he receives no health care or any other benefits; he lives in crowded quarters. Arturo doesn't speak English, though he has started attending a class offered by the local parish. He and his fellow workers are a group of vulnerable persons, willing to work hard in difficult circumstances, striving to improve their own lives and those of their families back home.

⊗⊗

The condition of workers was the issue that launched Catholic social teaching during the last decade of the nineteenth century. It remains one of the foremost concerns of the church early in the twenty-first century. Pope Leo XIII gave us the first social encyclical and it focused directly upon the situation of laborers adjusting to the harsh working conditions following the industrialization of Europe and North America. This attention to the struggles and rights of workers has endured throughout the one hundred plus years of papal social documents. In 1981 Pope John Paul II also devoted an entire encyclical to this topic, On Human Work. In this country the United States Conference of Catholic Bishops issues an annual Labor Day statement reflecting on an issue of contemporary importance to working people. Within this continuing emphasis on labor issues two topics receive priority consideration: the dignity of work and the rights of workers. Both topics are immediately relevant to Arturo and to all other workers anywhere in the world.

Human Work

One of the least understood aspects of Catholic social teaching is what it tells us about the nature and purpose of work. Most often we tend to associate this teaching with the rights and responsibilities of workers and employers. Certainly the teachings address this topic in considerable detail, but they have much to say as well about work itself, especially regarding the connection between work and the development of the human person. In a culture and an era when many look upon their jobs as little more than a necessary burden, the church's teaching on work presents alternative views worthy of our attention.

Why do we work?

At one time or another most of us probably have thought about work as a necessary evil, something we must do in order to put food on the table and a roof over our heads. Perhaps we have dreamed about retiring early or winning a big lottery so that we might be freed from this necessary burden we call work. Catholic social teaching looks at work quite differently. The church regards work as a fundamental dimension of our existence on earth (On Human Work, 4). Work is not an evil; it is a good thing for humans because through work we not only meet our daily needs but also achieve fulfillment as human beings (9). The teaching speaks of human work as both necessary and personal.

Work is necessary because in fact we do need to meet our daily needs. Without income it is difficult to secure food or any other basic necessities required for a dignified life. For most of us this income is obtained through work. We work also to provide for the needs of our families or any persons who are dependent upon us. This is Arturo's primary reason for separating himself from his home and his culture and accepting the work of milking cows in a strange land. He wants to improve living conditions for his family living in an economically depressed state in southern Mexico.

Beyond meeting personal needs, work is necessary to enable us to support the communities in which we live. Through work-related income taxes we contribute to the common good, to the well-being of our nation and to all of humanity. This sense of the moral necessity of work is presented by Pope John Paul II in his encyclical, On Human Work.

> Man must work out of regard for others, especially his own family, but also for the society he belongs to, the country of which he is a child and the whole human family of which he is a member, since he is the heir to the work of generations and at the same time a sharer in building the future of those who will come after him in the succession of history. All this constitutes the moral obligation of work, understood in its wide sense. (16)

Later, in his final social document, the pontiff expanded on the public character of work: "More than ever, work is work with others and work for others; it is a matter of doing something for someone else. Work becomes ever more fruitful and productive to the extent that people become . . . more profoundly cognizant of the needs of those for whom their work is done" (On the Hundredth Anniversary, 31).

To say that work is necessary is to acknowledge that we provide for our needs and those of our family through whatever job we have. The necessity of work points also to our need to contribute to the building and maintenance of healthy communities, societies, and living conditions worldwide.

Work is also personal. It is one of the ways in which we exercise the "distinctive human capacity for self-expression and self-realization" (Economic Justice for All, 97). The Second Vatican Council summarized this teaching on the personal nature of work:

> For when man works, he not only alters things and society, he develops himself as well. He learns much, he cultivates his resources, he goes outside of himself and beyond himself. (The Church in the Modern World, 35)

Work is so much more than "making a living." It is where we develop the gifts and talents that God has given us. It is where we utilize these gifts to meet our own needs and to improve the world about us. Work is an important manner of acknowledging that our abilities and skills are God's gifts to be used through us on behalf of all God's people. What we do at work, what we produce, how we relate to co-workers—all of this is an opportunity for responding to God's love for us and for learning how to be in right relationship with our neighbors. Through our work we learn how to take responsibility for our lives and moving forward in the journey of becoming whom God has called us to be. It hardly needs mentioning that wages and working conditions are a major factor in determining whether or not workers are able to experience this growth, to realize their dignity.

Learning responsibility

Because of this personal dimension of work, it is important that workers be engaged and committed to their place of work. It should be a place, an activity, and an experience that allows workers to develop themselves. Pope John XXIII regarded as justifiable the desire of employees to have some kind of partnership status in their places of work (Christianity and Social Progress, 91). The goal here is to foster working conditions that help to develop among the workers a sense of responsibility. He quoted Pope Pius XII on ways in which this might happen: "Small and medium-sized holdings in agriculture, in the arts and crafts, in commerce and industry, should be safeguarded and fostered" (84). Smaller places of employment, he believed, are more likely to create opportunities for employees to be engaged in the operation of the enterprise. Developing this sense of responsibility among workers in larger enterprises might happen by offering some kind of partnership arrangement to employees.

It is important to recognize that John XXIII, and Catholic social teaching generally, is not advocating one economic system over another. The concern is that in any economic system or structure the dignity of workers is honored. One way to do that is by allowing employees the opportunity to grow in responsibility for themselves, for others around them, and for the entire workplace. If workers are empowered to take on greater responsibilities within their places of employment, that is likely to carry over to the larger community. "But it should be emphasized how necessary, or at least very appropriate, it is to give workers an opportunity to exert influence outside the limits of the individual productive unit, and indeed within all ranks of the commonwealth" (Christianity and Social Progress, 97).

Pope Pius XI earlier had raised the desirability of workers gaining some kind of partnership status when he wrote in On Reconstructing the Social Order:

> [T]he wage contract should, when possible, be modified somewhat by a contract of partnership, as is already being tried in various ways with significant advantage to both wage earners and employers. For thus the workers and executives become sharers in the ownership or management, or else participate in some way in the profits. (65)

At the time, this statement gave rise to considerable discussion about whether the church was advocating some form of communal ownership of the means of production. It seems fair to say that this teaching is concerned less about the structure of ownership and more about how the system functions in relationship to the workers. Are the fruits of production allowed to accumulate in the hands of the wealthy or does "a sufficient and ample portion go to the workingmen?" (Christianity and Social Progress, 77). Most importantly, does the structure and functioning of the workplace promote among workers the development of a sense of responsibility for their own lives, for the enterprise itself, and for the larger communities in which they live?

For Pope John Paul II this could happen by "associating labor with the ownership of capital," by allowing the worker "to consider himself a part-owner of the great workbench at which he is working with everyone else" (On Human Work, 14). Again, the issue here is not the appropriate structure of ownership, but how that structure fosters the full development of the workers. Speaking of the purpose of ownership, John Paul II stressed how the means of production must be in service to workers.

> [T]he only legitimate title to their possession—whether in the form of private ownership or in the form of public or collective ownership—is that they should serve labor and thus by serving labor that they should make possible the achievement of the first principle of this order, namely the universal destination of goods and the right to common use of them. (On Human Work, 14)

Work's value

Catholic social teaching consistently reminds us that the economy, or any other structure of society, must serve people. If an economic or health care or educational system functions in such a way as to exclude significant numbers of people from its benefits, that system must be changed. The same attitude is present in how we regard work.

The value of work is found not primarily in the kind of work being done, nor even in what may be produced from the labor. The basis for evaluating human work is the fact that the one doing the work is a person; the one doing the work is more important than the work being done. The degree to which this work contributes to the self-realization of the person becomes the criterion for judging what is right and wrong about the work (On Human Work, 6). The value of one's job is not measured only or even primarily by what one does, nor by how important this job is for society, nor by how much it pays.

All of these considerations are important and they do say something about the value of the work or job. Nonetheless, the most important measure for determining the value of any work is the dignity this work gives to the person carrying it out. The work of a parking lot attendant is as valuable as that of a heart surgeon if the attendant's employer respects her dignity and allows her to develop her own sense of responsibility and serve others. On the same basis, Arturo's job among the cattle is as important as that of a molecular biologist involved in genetic engineering related to food production.

It is from this perspective that Catholic teaching insists that work has two essential dimensions. Not only is work necessary to make a living and to be a contributing member of society. Work also is personal. It is one of the major areas of our lives where we realize our sacred dignity and where we can practice the implications of that dignity by developing and using the gifts with which God has blessed each of us. This should be possible in any job, in any kind of work.

A just society

The condition of workers is a measure of the justice of a society. The social documents point out that persons must find in their work experience an opportunity to take on responsibility and to move forward in their own development. This is as important as the just distribution of wealth within a society.

> Consequently, if the organization and structure of economic life be such that the human dignity of workers is compromised, or their sense of responsibility is weakened, or their freedom of action is removed, then we judge such an economic order to be unjust, even

though it produces a vast amount of goods, whose distribution conforms to the norms of justice and equity. (Christianity and Social Progress, 83)

In his major encyclical on this topic of human work, Pope John Paul II leaves no doubt regarding the connection between labor issues and a just society. He writes that "there is something wrong with the organization of work and employment" when high numbers of people are unemployed or underemployed and many others suffer from hunger (On Human Work, 18). Compensation for work is the practical means by which the majority of people are able to have access to those goods they need for a dignified life. All these goods, we should remember, were meant by the Creator to satisfy the needs of everyone. In modern society these goods become accessible to workers through the wages they receive in return for their labor. "It should also be noted that the justice of a socioeconomic system and, in each case, its just functioning, deserve in the final analysis to be evaluated by the way in which man's work is properly remunerated in the system" (19).

Pope John Paul II sees human work as "the essential key to the whole social question." The gradual solution to this social question is found in the struggle to make life more human, and that can happen only when human work is regarded with fundamental and decisive importance (On Human Work, 3). Respect for the rights of all workers is the guiding norm for shaping and directing a nation's entire economy. National economic policies, such as taxation and minimum wage, influence how well individual enterprises respect their employees. The web of international economic relationships, such as the North American Free Trade Agreement (NAFTA) or World Trade Organization (WTO) agreements, greatly determine the extent to which employers in developing nations do or do not respect the rights of their workers.

Workers' Rights

In his discussion of rights and obligations, Pope John XXIII devoted considerable attention to economic or work-related rights (Peace on Earth, 18–22). These rights, he stressed, were particularly necessary to enable workers to care for themselves and their dependents and to contribute responsibly to the well-being of the larger community. Catholic social documents before and after Peace on Earth have devoted considerable attention to questions about labor and the rights of workers. Among the rights of employees, three especially stand out as necessary for the protection of human dignity: the right to suitable employment, to just wages, and to collective bargaining.

Satisfactory work

In his comprehensive discussion of human rights, Pope John XXIII began his treatment of economic rights by noting that every person should be granted an opportunity for work (Peace on Earth, 18). Clearly this position is based on a prior recognition that every person capable of doing so should work. As noted earlier, work is the normal way for most persons to earn their living, to care for dependents, and to contribute to the common good. Work is necessary and it is personal. It is one way in which we develop ourselves as responsible persons made in the image of God.

If everyone is expected to work, then the opportunity to do so must be provided. Unemployment and underemployment make it extremely difficult for some within the work force to satisfy this expectation to work. Lack of satisfactory employment easily becomes an obstacle to the realization of human dignity. It also harms society at large through loss of taxes and revenues, and through increased unemployment compensation and public assistance needs.

Catholic teaching regards unemployment, "which in all cases is an evil" (On Human Work, 18), quite differently from some economists who argue that the capitalist economic system functions best with a certain rate of unemployment. If the economists are right, then from a Catholic perspective, the economic system must be changed. This is an example of the need for structural or institutional change embedded in the notion of social justice. Pope John Paul II summarized this teaching while discussing the duties of those who own the means of production.

> The obligation to earn one's bread by the sweat of one's brow also presumes the right to do so. A society in which this right is systematically denied, in which economic policies do not allow workers to reach satisfactory levels of employment, cannot be justified from an ethical point of view, nor can that society attain social peace. (On the Hundredth Anniversary, 43)

He concludes by noting that ownership justifies itself morally by creating the "opportunities for work and human growth."

Just wages

From time to time state legislatures and the United States Congress consider raising the minimum wage. Law makers often decide not to increase this wage because of perceived negative impacts such action will have on the economy. Wherever the minimum wage stands, it always remains below what is needed for workers to rise above the poverty level. If a person today receiving the minimum wage works full time, fifty-two weeks of the year with no vacation or sick leave, that person remains several thousand dollars below the poverty level. In the United States today more than a million full-time employees remain in poverty. In no aspect of labor issues does Catholic social teaching challenge current practice more than on the topic of what constitutes a just wage.

Pope Pius XI stated the church's position in its simplest form when he wrote in 1931 that a wage paid to a worker should be sufficient to support him and his family (On Reconstructing the Social Order, 71). Although later social teachings present criteria for determining a just wage, the focus always remains upon the worker, the one who receives the wage. The worker must be paid enough to enable her along with her family to live a dignified life, what Leo XIII referred to as a wage "sufficient to enable him to maintain himself, his wife, and his children in reasonable comfort" (On the Condition of Labor, 35). Wages, in other words, must enable the worker to obtain what is needed to live decently: food, housing, health care, education, etc. There can be no doubt that for millions of workers in the United States, the minimum wage provides no such assurance.

The church's teaching on a just wage is an example of how some of the social teachings have developed over the decades. In this case, the core of the teaching remains unchanged—a just wage is one that enables workers and their dependents to live a dignified life. What has changed or developed are the additional factors to be considered in determining what constitutes the just wage. That includes the contribution of each worker as well as the economic condition of the employer. John XXIII added that the "requirements of each community, especially as regards overall employment" (Christianity and Social Progress, 71) must be considered. Finally, a just wage should be determined in light of the general common good. None of this means giving less attention to the needs of the workers themselves. It simply suggests that in arriving at a decision regarding what workers should be paid—especially when it is beyond meeting basic needs—other factors enter. The Second Vatican Council summarized the church's teaching on the just wage.

Finally, payment for labor must be such as to furnish a man with the means to cultivate his own material, social, cultural, and spiritual life worthily, and that of his dependents. What this payment should be will vary according to each man's assignment and productivity, the conditions of his place of employment, and the common good. (The Church in the Modern World, 67)

The ultimate test of a just wage is whether it provides the income for a worker to live a decent life. If it does not meet this test—even though the worker has agreed to work for this less than adequate pay—it is not a just wage. Leo XIII wrote that employer and worker should come to an agreement about all aspects of the job, especially the wages the employee will receive. In spite of such agreements, however, there is a more basic "dictate of nature" that calls for an adequate wage and that overrides any agreement between employer and worker. "If through necessity or fear of a worse evil, the workman accepts harder conditions because an employer or contractor will give him no better, he is the victim of force and injustice" (On the Condition of Labor, 34).

Migrant workers, as well as recent immigrants like Arturo, sometimes find themselves in the vulnerable position of having to accept what is offered or being without work. This vulnerability is heightened for those whose entrance into the United States is not properly documented. None of this, not even the worker's acceptance of unfair labor terms, justifies an employer's refusal to provide just wages and benefits along with safe working conditions. Pope Leo acknowledged that it is not always easy to determine whether a wage is adequate, yet he warned employers against mistreatment of workers.

[R]ich men and masters should remember this—that to exercise pressure for the sake of gain, upon the indigent and destitute, and to make one's profit out of the need of another, is condemned by all laws, human and divine. To defraud any one of wages that are his due is a crime which cries to the avenging anger of heaven [Jas 5:4]. (On the Condition of Labor, 17)

So important is this question of the just wage that Pope John Paul II claimed it as the standard by which to evaluate "the justice of a socio-economic system." This, John Paul continued, is simply recognizing "the first principle of the whole ethical and social order, namely the principle of the common use of goods" (On Human Work, 19). Just wages normally assure access to those goods needed to live a dignified life.

Unions

One of the means available to workers to help secure a just wage is the labor union. The very first social encyclical near the end of the nineteenth century recognized the right of workers to form unions to represent employees collectively in bargaining with employers. On the Condition of Labor approved of such associations, and it did so at a time when many church leaders felt that Catholic workers should belong only to "confessional associations," unions organized by and for Catholic workers. Responding to the entreaties of an American cardinal, John Gibbons of Baltimore, Pope Leo XIII recognized the right of all workers to form workmen's associations—later called unions—and to organize them in whatever manner best provides for the needs of workers and the protection of their rights (On the Condition of Labor, 42).

The social documents that followed Leo XIII all reiterated the legitimate right of workers to join together in unions to defend their interests in all matters related to their employment. Pope John Paul II noted the need for workers themselves to secure their rights. Unions, therefore, are an "indispensable element of social life, especially in modern industrialized societies" (On Human Work, 20). The United States Catholic bishops see contemporary anti-union efforts as an assault on human dignity.

> No one may deny the right to organize without attacking human dignity itself. Therefore, we firmly oppose organized efforts, such as those regrettably now seen in this country, to break existing unions and prevent workers from organizing. (Economic Justice for All, 104)

Labor unions engage in a number of activities to protect the interests of workers. None is quite so controversial as the strike. The history of the labor movement in the United States and Canada records its share of violent confrontations that accompanied some of the early strikes. This was part of the reason for the Vatican's condemnation of the Knights of Labor in Quebec prior to the papacy of Leo XIII. This was also the reason for Leo's reluctance to approve of Catholic workers joining mixed unions (both Catholic and non-Catholic workers).

When Leo finally did approve such unions, he nonetheless expressed deep reservations about the strike, noting that it harms both trade and the general interests of the public. Violence often accompanies the strike, bringing disorder and threatening public peace. "The laws should be made beforehand, and prevent these troubles from arising; they should lend their influence and authority to the removal in good time of the causes which lead to conflicts between masters and those whom they employ" (On the Condition of Labor, 31). Although Leo refrains from directly endorsing the strike, he does recognize that unions must be permitted to function in a way to provide the "best and most suitable means for attaining what is aimed at," namely the protection of the rights of workers (42).

The successors of Leo XIII were far more willing to recognize both the necessity and the legitimacy of labor strikes. John Paul II summarizes this teaching in his encyclical On Human Work. He specifically states that the strike or work stoppage is a method for pursuing the just rights of workers that is "recognized by Catholic social teaching as legitimate in the proper conditions and within just limits" (20). He adds that the strike, though legitimate, should be employed as an extreme means, a kind of ultimatum to employers. The just limits of a strike would include making sure that the work stoppage does not threaten essential community services. Nor should a strike be used in a way that paralyzes the socioeconomic life of society.

While unions have a specific role securing the rights of workers, this task must be carried out with an eye to the good of the whole society. Unions must never seek their goals at the expense of the common good, nor should they see their mission as part of a class struggle. John Paul II describes the kind of struggle to which unions are rightly committed. He reminds us that unions are engaged in the struggle for social justice. Like any social justice effort, the challenge for unions is to bring structural changes to protect the rights of certain individuals. It is an effort on behalf of the common good. The United States Catholic bishops took up this point in Economic Justice for All, noting that workers should use their collective bargaining power not only for their personal interests, but also for the well-being of the whole community. Never should unions press for demands that would harm the common good or make life more difficult for those in society who are more vulnerable.

At the same time, the bishops point out that wages—so often the focus of union demands—are but one of the factors affecting the competitive stance of an industry. "Thus, it is unfair to expect unions to make concessions if managers and shareholders do not make at least equal sacrifices" (106).

It is the task of unions to help workers achieve a position in which they are able to make contributions to their own workplace and to their communities. They do this by developing within workers a sense of their own responsibility for the well-being of the larger society. The Second Vatican Council reflected on the kind of social commitment that unions should foster among workers: "Thus they will be brought to feel that according to their own proper capacities and aptitudes they are associates in the whole task of economic and social development and in the attainment of the universal common good" (The Church in the Modern World, 68).

Protecting the Dignity of Work and the Rights of Workers

Protecting the rights of workers—to satisfactory work, to just wages, to collective bargaining—is an essential aspect of honoring and defending the dignity of workers. These rights are as important as any others found in Catholic social teaching's first discussion of human rights (Peace on Earth, 11–27). Protecting workers' rights also is a way of recognizing the dignity of work. It is an acknowledgement that through their work human beings use the gifts received from the Creator to develop themselves and direct their energies to the service of brothers and sisters. Work, therefore, is a human activity to be valued highly. We do so by protecting the rights of those who work and by respecting the formative power of work itself.

Role of the state

Workers, employers, and society as a whole have a responsibility to maintain work as the dignified human activity it can and should be. This is not the task of employees alone. Within society the state has a particular role in this endeavor. One of the responsibilities of government is to defend human dignity and to protect all human rights, including those related to work. It is also the duty of government to promote the common good, to create those conditions of social living by which all members of society can achieve their fulfillment. Employment is a major part of that social living.

It is the role of the state to protect the rights of workers to unionize, to safe working conditions, to just wages, and to satisfactory work.

Catholic social teaching has stated consistently that everyone has a right to employment. Securing adequate work for all is the responsibility of everyone, including government. "Then the burden of securing full employment falls on all of us—policy makers, business, labor, and the general public—to create and implement the mechanisms to protect that right" (Economic Justice for All, 153).

One of the more general expectations of government regarding work is that it will take measures to ensure satisfactory employment for all who can work. Another governmental responsibility in this area, one focused on a more specific segment of the labor force today, is to look after the needs of migrant agricultural workers. Speaking directly to the situation in the United States, the bishops stress that migrant workers in agriculture have been and remain a particularly vulnerable part of our work force. Arturo and his friends working on the dairy farm enjoy stationary employment, but their conditions are similar to those endured by migrants. All of these workers are in need of protection, especially in such areas as exercising their right to collective bargaining. The bishops point out that some of these unfair labor practices can be addressed most effectively through labor law.

Role of the church

The church also has responsibilities related to labor. Its social teachings on the rights of workers and the dignity of work represent an important contribution to society's understanding of work. Prophetic denunciations of the abuse of workers' rights can help shape the labor climate and disseminate the teachings. The church has a long history of speaking out in defense of workers—the first social encyclical, the annual Labor Day statement, the support of unionizing efforts among the United Farm Workers of America. All of this points to the mission of the church, a religious mission to be sure, but a mission out of which comes both a light and energy to help structure the human community (The Church in the Modern World, 42). The manner in which humans structure every aspect of society has its impact upon how well each member of society realizes his or her dignity. Nowhere in the organization of economic structures is this more important than in the just treatment of workers.

The church's social teachings and prophetic statements bear witness to these beliefs. The church's own actions determine how well these teachings and statements are received, as noted by the World Synod of Bishops:

> While the Church is bound to give witness to justice, she recognizes that everyone who ventures to speak to people about justice, must first be just in their eyes. (Justice in the World, 40)

What Catholic social teaching says about the rights of workers is meant for all workers, including persons employed by the church. The bishops at the World Synod also noted that "No one should be deprived of his ordinary rights because he is associated with the church in one way or another" (41). Clergy, religious, and lay people all should be given fair wages and all other rights that Catholic social teaching recognizes for workers. This includes the right to unionize. "All church institutions must also fully recognize the rights of employees to organize and bargain collectively with the institution through whatever association or organization they freely choose" (Economic Justice for All, 353).

Discussion

1. In your experience, how do most people look at work? How do these views compare with Catholic social teaching regarding the meaning and value of work?

2. How often do you think about your work as a means of using God's gifts in service to others? Is it possible to see your job in this way? Why or why not?

3. Catholic social teaching claims that respecting the dignity of work and the rights of workers is a yardstick for measuring the justice of our society. How is the United States doing?

4. If another person asks you to explain what Catholic social teaching means by "the dignity of work," how will you respond?

Actions

1. Visit a county or city jobs assistance office and ask about employment conditions in the area—typical wages, benefits, unionizing.

2. Interview three persons with very different jobs—e.g., a factory worker, a teacher, a doctor. Ask them how they view their jobs. Do any of them reflect Catholic social teaching regarding the dignity of work?

3. Visit your diocesan personnel office and ask about employment policies, especially regarding wages, health care, and retirement. Does your parish follow these policies?

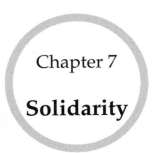

Chapter 7

Solidarity

Father Jack has been in Chimbote for more than thirty years. This city in northern Peru is home to some of the world's worst poverty. Since he became pastor of Our Lady of Perpetual Help, Father Jack has initiated numerous programs to help the 30,000 people in this parish—soup kitchens, construction and employment programs, child care, shelters for battered women, tutoring classes, a medical clinic, activities for physically and mentally handicapped persons, and a beautiful hospice. Perhaps his most important project is making connections between the people in his parish and people in the United States and other countries. Father Jack has established several sister parish relationships and has nurtured ties with several thousand people around the world. Because of these relationships, he is able to support the various programs that bring food, medicine, jobs, education, and dignity to the gentle people of Chimbote. As important as the money, Father Jack's efforts bring to Chimbote visitors from the United States and other places, many returning again and again. Whether they stay for a week or a year, these guests learn how so many people have to live with so few resources. They also experience their own connectedness to a people who, in spite of poverty and sickness, are able to express a Christ-like love and hospitality to one another and to their guests. Few leave Chimbote without a sense of compassion and solidarity for the beautiful people who have cared for them during their visit.

৩৩

During his long term as pope, John Paul II contributed much to the development of one core theme in Catholic social teaching—solidarity. The word rarely appears in documents written before 1978 when Karl Wojtyla was elected pontiff. It first gained public attention not within church structures but in the labor organizing effort of a Polish workers' union. Not surprisingly, Cardinal Wojtyla supported the Polish labor organizers as they drew inspiration from Catholic social teaching on the rights of workers. As pope, John Paul II developed the theme of solidarity far beyond the sphere of labor organizing.

One Human Family

Documents written prior to those of John Paul II laid the foundation for solidarity with their basic teaching on the common good. There is one human family and each member of that family bears a responsibility for the well-being of other members, especially those who are close in terms of family, friends, and geographical area. By the time of the Second Vatican Council it was well established that an individualistic morality does not satisfy one's obligations of justice and love. Nor is it an adequate response to our call to communion with God. The Council reminded us that

> it has pleased God to make men holy and save them not merely as individuals, without any mutual bonds, but by making them into a single people, a people which acknowledges him in truth and serves him in holiness. (The Church in the Modern World, 32)

Universal common good

We satisfy our duties of justice and love in part by reaching out to others and by contributing to the common good—by fostering "those conditions of social life by which individuals, families, and groups can achieve their own fulfillment in a relatively thorough and ready way" (The Church in the Modern World, 74). How we do that and to what extent will vary from one person to another depending upon our circumstances, our resources, and the needs of others. What is clear in Catholic social teaching is that every human being has something to offer to the building up of the human family. The talents that God has placed in each of us for that purpose must be developed and utilized in our work, families, and communities.

The Second Vatican Council also brought a stronger challenge. It noted that our thinking about the common good no longer can be restricted to national boundaries. Today it takes on a universal complexion involving rights and duties in relation to this global human family. It is not enough to consider our personal needs or those of our family. "Every social group must take account of the needs and legitimate aspirations of other groups, and even of the general welfare of the human family" (The Church in the Modern World, 26). Today the fulfillment of our responsibilities to the common good takes us beyond our own communities and even our own nation. The well-being of the entire human race must enter into our deliberations about what is best for our society. The experience of visiting Father Jack's parish in Peru awakens in anyone a compassion not limited by geographical borders.

Solidarity as a virtue

This concern for the entire global community is what John Paul II later called the Christian virtue of solidarity. It is closely aligned with charity, "the distinguishing mark of Christ's disciples" (On Social Concern, 40). He notes that solidarity, like charity, reaches beyond itself and reflects the gratitude, forgiveness, and reconciliation expected from those who follow Christ. Through solidarity we look upon our neighbors, both near and far, as the living images of God, as persons redeemed by Christ and guided by the Spirit to communion with God. Through solidarity we are able to see all humans as made in the image and likeness of God and enjoying the same dignity and rights that we claim for ourselves.

In Catholic theology we speak of virtues as ongoing or "habitual dispositions" to do good. This virtue of solidarity is no different. It means that we take on the attitude of seeing our connectedness to all other humans. It means that we nurture—as a habit—this posture of embracing our membership in the one human family. Most importantly, it means that we continually live and act in ways that reflect our dependence upon and responsibility for all of God's children anywhere in the world.

The practical implications of solidarity are stunning. We must love our neighbor with the same love that Christ has shown for all of us. We must love even our enemies this way. Pope John Paul II wrote that this kind of love, the love of Christ, prepares us to sacrifice even to the point of giving our lives for our neighbor (On Social Concern, 40). One of the challenges to living this virtue of solidarity today is the justification of war against our neighbors who in spite of seriously wrong actions present to us "the living image of God."

The U.S. Catholic bishops reflect on additional challenges to living in solidarity with others, especially persons less well off.

> Solidarity is action on behalf of the one human family, calling us to help overcome the divisions in our world. Solidarity binds the rich to the poor. It makes the free zealous for the cause of the oppressed. It drives the comfortable and secure to take risks for the victims of tyranny and war. It calls for those who are strong to care for those who are weak and vulnerable across the spectrum of human life. It opens homes and hearts to those in flight from terror and to migrants whose daily toil supports affluent lifestyles. Peacemaking, as Pope John Paul II has told us, is the work of solidarity. (Called to Global Solidarity, 4)

Solidarity, like any virtue, calls for action. It may be a timely act to assist a person in need, active participation in war resistance activities, or an ongoing effort to change our lifestyles so we are capable of responding to others. In any case, to be in solidarity with others is to recognize our shared human dignity, our one human family, and to act accordingly.

Our Brothers' and Sisters' Keepers

Catholic social teaching enjoys a strong foundation in the Scriptures and in early Christian writing. There probably is no stronger ethical teaching in these biblical and patristic texts than the call to love our neighbor and to show that love through practical actions. The Letter of James questions how anyone who refuses to help another person in need can possibly have faith. Christian writers of the first few centuries held that to refuse food to a person dying of hunger is to share in the guilt of that person's death. Solidarity calls us to respond to the needs of others and to do so in concrete, helpful ways.

Linked and limited world

The contemporary emphasis upon solidarity in Catholic social teaching parallels a growing awareness of the interdependencies and limitations in our world. In 1997 the Catholic bishops of the United States commented that globalization in economics, transportation, and communication have drawn the world together, while at the same time bringing benefits to a few while impoverishing many. "The gulf between rich and poor nations has widened, and the sense of responsibility toward the world's poor and oppressed has grown weaker. The world watched for too long as thousands died in Bosnia, Rwanda, and Zaire" (Called to Global Solidarity, 2).

Twenty years later that list might include the Sudan and Niger—countries suffering from genocide and famine as the rest of the world fails to respond. These words remind us of the lament of Pope Paul VI forty years ago when he stated that no longer can one be ignorant of the fact that whole continents are ravaged by hunger and condemned to the most depressing living conditions (On the Development of Peoples, 45). Solidarity is in the forefront because we know that millions of people now suffer from unnecessary poverty and oppression. We know the extent of their suffering as well as the circumstances from which it arises. We always have known that Christ's command to love our neighbor as ourselves means all of our neighbors. Today in a world we know to be so connected and yet so limited, Jesus' command to love carries particularly strong global implications. This awareness can be both an opportunity and an indictment. It is an opportunity to respond to peoples' immediate needs and to try to change whatever causes their suffering. Awareness becomes an indictment when, in spite of what we know, we refuse to act. At the start of the twenty-first century the wonders of information technology make us more aware of stressful, painful situations around the globe than at any time in human history. We are our brothers' and sisters' keepers and we are called to action on behalf of justice without regard for national boundaries.

Responsible for all

The increasing sense of global connectedness—a dimension of the virtue of solidarity—arises in part from our expanding knowledge of the needs and aspirations of people everywhere. It grows also out of every nation's recognition that its own hope for a good life is dependent upon people in all parts of the world. Solidarity, then, is not simply a feeling of compassion or pity for persons who are suffering. Nor does it move in only one direction. It is, as Pope John Paul II stated, an enduring commitment to the good of everyone and of every individual person and of every nation because "we are all really responsible for all" (On Social Concern, 38).

Through this virtue of solidarity we are empowered to see all other persons, groups, and nations as our neighbors and helpers. We recognize the one human family that we are, and we celebrate the unique gifts that each person, each culture and each nation brings to this family's journey to God. As Pope John Paul II stated in his "Message for the World Day of Peace" in 2000, the spirit of solidarity leads us to see the poor "not as a problem, but as people who can become the principle builders of a new and more human future for everyone" (Peace on Earth to Those Whom God Loves, 14). Father Jack challenges his parishioners. In staff meetings and especially in preaching he urges them to understand the causes of their poverty and to recognize their own gifts for confronting and changing some of the factors that contribute to their difficult life.

Those of us in more affluent societies also need to appreciate the wisdom that other nations and cultures bring to the task of building a more humane world. Many of these peoples pursue lifestyles guided by values that inspire caring for neighbors, moderation in consumption, and living in proper relationship with the earth. Solidarity challenges us to live in the awareness of our connectedness to this human family, to respond generously to this family's needs anywhere, and to receive with humility and gratitude what this family can teach us about being human.

Seeking a Just Social Order

Solidarity leads us to look upon persons and nations as part of one global community sharing the same destiny and benefiting from the blessings and gifts that God has placed in each individual and country. This virtue also directs us to work for changes in the economic, political, and social structures that contribute to the poverty and oppression confronting millions of people around the globe.

Prosperity interdependent

Pope Paul VI reminded us that working for a more just social order contributes to improved living environments and to the complete, integral development of those who are the victims of poverty and injustice. "To wage war on misery and to struggle against injustice is to promote, along with improved conditions, the human and spiritual progress of all men, and therefore the common good of humanity" (On the Development of Peoples, 76). Clearly Paul VI saw such actions as benefiting not only those who suffer but those who work to relieve that suffering and to challenge whatever causes living conditions that dishonor human dignity. In that sense the spiritual growth of those who are better off is related to the economic improvements of those who are not. The common good of all humanity is enriched by the movement of any people from less to more humane living conditions. Pope John XXIII acknowledged this interdependent progress among nations when he wrote that the prosperity of any one nation is related in a dependent way to the prosperity of all the rest (Peace on Earth, 131). No single nation or block of nations can sustain long term prosperity at the expense or even the neglect of the development needs of other countries.

This interdependence among modern nations creates conditions favorable to the practice of solidarity. It leads to the recognition that the common good of my nation is served by considering the legitimate interests of other peoples and of the entire human family. This is a practical, almost utilitarian form of concern for others, and it may lead to public policies and relationships among nations that benefit everyone. Yet it falls short of the fullness of solidarity. The latter prompts us to consider the needs and interests of others simply because they are persons bearing the same human dignity and rights that we claim for ourselves. Anything we say about our own dignity and destiny, any rights we claim for ourselves in support of a dignified life—all of this we must be willing to grant to any other person in our own country or anywhere in the world. This entails a commitment on our part and a readiness to let go of what we possess.

Sacrifice

Pope John Paul II wrote that a way to promote reasonable prosperity and human development among all peoples is to live in a manner that makes resources available to all. "Interdependence must be transformed into solidarity, based on the principle that the goods of creation are meant for all. That which human industry produces through the processing of raw materials, with the contribution of work, must serve equally for the good of all" (On Social Concern, 39).

Any nation blessed with an abundance of natural resources must be willing to share these gifts in a reasonable manner with countries less endowed. Any nation steeped in manufactured material goods also must consider how such abundance might assist those nations unable to produce what is needed for their people. This obligation is grounded in the biblical teaching so clearly articulated by the early Christian writers that all of God's creation is here to satisfy the needs of everyone. This obligation rests on the practical realization that no nation can prosper indefinitely in a world where other nations suffer from lack of resources. This obligation emerges from the virtue of solidarity—from the habitual practice of recognizing that all of us on earth are children of the one God who calls us to himself and charges us to love one another along the way.

This is no abstraction. It summons us to choices about how we live and what kind of laws and public policies we support. As Pope John Paul II stated, solidarity requires "a concerted worldwide effort to promote development, an effort which also involves sacrificing the positions of income and of power enjoyed by the more developed economies" (On the Hundredth Anniversary, 52). This is the preferential option for the poor applied to the global level. It calls upon all of us to support economic relationships and trade agreements designed especially to help countries with the greatest needs.

Globalization

Today we hear much about globalization and its effects, especially economic, upon nations both rich and poor. It bears noting that various aspects of the current globalization process have been in motion for many decades. While difficult to define in a sentence, the practices of transnational corporations in seeking more favorable production conditions around the globe are one example of globalization. Global economic regulatory agencies such as the International Monetary Fund (IMF) and, more recently, the WTO, are also a part of this globalization process. Trade agreements like NAFTA in 1994 and the Central American Free Trade Agreement (CAFTA) in 2005 are but the latest examples of efforts by political and economic decision makers to extend globalization. However defined, its goals are clear: to remove barriers to the trading of commodities (natural and manufactured) as well as enhance the mobility of financial capital and labor across national boundaries. Less clear is how these developments will benefit countries with the greatest needs or even lower income workers in more affluent societies.

The virtue of solidarity in Catholic social teaching provides a perspective for evaluating this worldwide phenomenon, a perspective that draws especially from the church's teaching on participation as well as the option for the poor and the vulnerable. In his 1998 World Day of Peace message, Pope John Paul II spoke out against the new inequalities that accompany the globalization process.

> [W]e can no longer tolerate a world in which there live side by side the immensely rich and the miserably poor, the have-nots deprived even of essentials and people who thoughtlessly waste what others so desperately need. Such contrasts are an affront to the dignity of the human person. (From the Justice of Each Comes Peace for All, 4)

The Holy Father's observation is confirmed by the experience of thousands of people from the United States and other affluent societies who have spent time among Father Jack's parishioners in Chimbote. The benefits of globalization must not slip past the underprivileged who too often are excluded from social and economic progress. For that to happen, the less developed nations must have an equal voice in shaping the new economic arrangements. More, not fewer, people need to enter into decision-making processes related to the development of the world's new economic relationships. From the perspective of Catholic social teaching, the urgent need is to strive for what John Paul II referred to as a globalization without marginalization. That can happen if those with decision-making power focus upon the universal common good and create ways for all groups and nations to participate as equals in this newly emerging international economy.

Pope John Paul II recognized that globalization of the economy, which he regarded as a reality, can lead to opportunities for greater prosperity for everyone. "Globalization, for all its risks, also offers exceptional and promising opportunities, precisely with a view to enabling humanity to become a single family, built on the values of justice, equity and solidarity" (Peace on Earth, 5).

This requires effective international agencies invested with the necessary resources and power to direct this changing economy towards the common good. This is a task, he cautioned, that an individual nation, "even if it were the most powerful on earth, would not be in a position to do" (On the Hundredth Anniversary, 58). Solidarity calls us to commit ourselves to the well-being of all peoples and all nations. It requires as well that we identify and support the means by which solidarity might be achieved.

Subsidiarity

A discussion of solidarity may appear an unlikely context for discussing the principle of subsidiarity. Yet this principle, which is present at the very beginning of Catholic social teaching, is critical for living out the virtue of solidarity. This is particularly so when considering solidarity in relation to globalization. John Paul II summarizes a century of Catholic teaching on subsidiarity.

> [A] community of a higher order should not interfere in the internal life of a community of a lower order, depriving the latter of its functions, but rather should support it in case of need and help coordinate its activities with the rest of society, always with a view to the common good. (On the Hundredth Anniversary, 48)

The caution embedded in this principle is that larger entities should not do for individuals and smaller organizations what the latter are able to accomplish themselves. Stated more positively, larger authorities should take on an attitude of helping and supporting the smaller entities achieve their own goals and fulfill their responsibilities. The principle of subsidiarity presupposes that every person and organization has something to offer the larger community. It also claims, consistent with the meaning of human dignity, that all persons and organizations require sufficient freedom to be able to exercise initiative and responsibility in realizing their goals and responsibilities.

The principle of subsidiarity applies as much to relationships between nations as it does to those within nations, states, and local communities. In his encyclical, On Social Concern, Pope John Paul II stressed the need for developing nations to chart their own course towards development: "In order to take this path, the nations themselves will have to identify their own priorities and clearly recognize their own needs, according to the particular conditions of their people, their geographical setting, and their cultural traditions" (44).

The progress of any nation depends above all upon the capabilities of its people to respond to the needs of that country. Whatever economic trade or foreign assistance relationships a nation might enter, those relations must not diminish that country's ability to determine its own course. In the 1960s Pope Paul VI was particularly blunt in applying the principle of subsidiarity to nations receiving foreign assistance.

> And the receiving countries could demand that there be no interference in their political life or subversion of their social structures. As sovereign states they have the right to conduct their own affairs, to decide on their policies, and to move freely towards the kind of society they choose. (On the Development of Peoples, 54)

The virtue of solidarity guides us to do all we can to promote the progress of all other persons and nations anywhere in the world. The principle of subsidiarity tells us how we are to provide such help—by respecting the dignity of those we are helping, by fostering their greatest participation in their own development, and by helping to create conditions that require the exercise of their own freedom and responsibility.

Peace

Our world always seems to be at war. In recent decades the evening news carries countless stories about one country attacking another or about civil strife within nations, sometimes accompanied by acts of genocide, or about the ever-present fear of terrorist acts. Under this dark shadow it is worth considering the relationship between solidarity and the peace that all of us so desire. Pope John XXIII noted the increasing connections among all nations of the world. With greater contact comes more accurate knowledge of how people in other lands are living. Today it is impossible for the more affluent nations not to see the hunger, poverty, and suffering of those countries with whom they now have economic and political dealings. The reverse is equally true. The poor of the world become ever more conscious of how the affluent live.

Threatened by injustice

As nations increase their contacts and dependencies, as people in struggling countries become more aware of what they do not have, the preservation of lasting peace will be very difficult (Christianity and Social Progress, 157). Pope Paul VI repeated this warning when he stated that excessive inequalities among nations lead to tensions and conflicts that jeopardize peace (On the Development of Peoples, 76). Pope John Paul II summarized this thinking in even sharper language, observing that the growing demand for justice must be satisfied on a worldwide basis.

> To ignore this demand could encourage the temptation among the victims of injustice to respond with violence, as happens at the origin of many wars. Peoples excluded from the fair distribution of the goods originally destined for all could ask themselves: why not respond with violence to those who first treat us with violence? (On Social Concern, 10)

In that context John Paul II stressed that the way to peace is found in promoting the social, cultural, and economic development of all peoples.

War and even military preparations are "the major enemy" of this integral development (10). Peace will come when all peoples and all nations honor their calling by the Creator to be one human family, when all of us commit ourselves to living in solidarity. The Second Vatican Council had stated earlier that peace is not secured by maintaining a balance of power between enemies. Rather, peace is "an enterprise of justice" (The Church in the Modern World, 78).

The fruit of justice and solidarity

Paul VI added that peace is more than the absence of war, especially if such a state results from a dangerous balance of power among potential combatants. Peace is built up day after day. It results from an intentional effort to pursue that order intended by God, an order in which all of us seek to live in proper relationship with God, with our neighbors throughout the world, and with all of God's creation. This is a peace that is rooted in an ever-developing form of justice among people (On the Development of Peoples, 76). It is guided by our practice of the virtue of solidarity, our constant effort to see all other people as our brothers and sisters in the one human family. John Paul II drew the connection between justice and solidarity as the cornerstones of lasting peace. Reflecting on Pope Pius XII's motto, "Peace as the fruit of justice," John Paul II asserted that today we could say with equal accuracy and biblical inspiration, "Peace as the fruit of solidarity" (On Social Concern, 39).

Such a peace rises out of the mutual trust that develops between nations, a trust which is the fruit of our desire to seek the common good of all peoples (The Church in the Modern World, 82). It can never result from fear of another's weapons or from a readiness to employ moral criteria that justify the march to war. Peace is the fruit of justice and solidarity. It rises from the efforts of each of us to seek the good of all—all peoples and all nations (From the Justice of Each Comes Peace for All, 7). Justice means being faithful to the expectations of our relationships. Today those relationships are global, and our faithfulness to those relationships determines any hope we may have for peace. The U.S. Catholic bishops stated in the mid-1980s that working for peace is part of our identity as followers of Jesus Christ.

> Peacemaking is not an optional commitment. It is a requirement of our faith. We are called to be peacemakers, not by some movement of the moment, but by our Lord Jesus. (The Challenge of Peace, 333)

Everyone's Responsibility

Solidarity is the way to peace and to the kind of development that promotes peace. The practice of this virtue promises to turn distrust and tension among peoples into collaboration and a desire to see improvements in living conditions for those who suffer. Pope John Paul II reminds us that solidarity contributes to the building of just relationships on all levels of human interaction—among individuals, within nations, and across international boundaries (On Social Concern, 40).

All nations

Catholic social teaching has recognized that the practice of solidarity on the international level can be aided by the existence and functioning of a global authority. Already in the 1960s Pope John XXIII noted that the universal common good required a public authority endowed with the necessary structure, resources, and power to deal effectively with the challenges of development and peace across the globe (Peace on Earth, 137). His successor gave greater specificity to this idea. Paul VI wrote of the need for a world fund to assist needed development. He noted the problem of world debts and the danger of international aid offered in a manner that interferes with the receiving nation's political life or undermines its social structures. He called for new approaches to trade relations. He concluded these reflections on justice, peace, and solidarity by repeating what he had stated during a visit to the existing global authority.

> "Your vocation," as we said to the representatives of the United Nations in New York, "is to bring not some people but all peoples to treat each other as brothers. . . . Who does not see the necessity of thus establishing progressively a world authority, capable of acting effectively in the juridical and political sectors?" (On the Development of Peoples, 78)

One of the responsibilities of this world authority is to lead the effort to help economically weaker nations to move beyond a subsistence level and to become more active and participatory members of the community of nations. Catholic teaching on social justice applies equally to individuals and to nations. All nations must contribute to the universal common good, but conditions of poverty or lack of resources often prevent one or more countries from making such contributions.

That is where other nations, especially under the leadership of an international authority, must seek to bring changes that will empower weaker nations to move forward. These changes may take the form of greater humanitarian aid, development assistance, or restructured trade relations. Their goal is to empower struggling nations to make their own contributions to the common good and to do so with the treasures of their own nations and cultures (On Social Concern, 39).

This approach to international cooperation respects the dignity of all people in the world. Equally important, it honors the right and responsibility of every nation to be equal partners in building a world community which strives to reflect the body of that new human family, "a body which even now is able to give some kind of foreshadowing of the new age" (The Church in the Modern World, 39). Through the practice of the virtue of solidarity we come to appreciate the wonderful truth that even the poorest of nations has something to contribute to the world community—a truth easily grasped by spending even a brief time among the people of Chimbote.

The church

Members of the Catholic Church have a particularly strong calling to solidarity. The teachings of the church and the many programs provide both theoretical directions and practical opportunities to learn what it means to practice the virtue of solidarity. John Paul II followed a line of church leaders who have taught consistently that the church stands beside the poor as part of her evangelical duty (On Social Concern, 39). Decades earlier the World Synod of Bishops left no doubt about the importance of working for justice as part of the church's mission.

> Action on behalf of justice and participation in the transformation of the world fully appear to us as a constitutive dimension of the preaching of the Gospel, or, in other words, of the Church's mission for the redemption of the human race and its liberation from every oppressive situation. (Justice in the World, 6)

The church's first task is to proclaim Jesus Christ—his name, his life, his teachings, the Kingdom that he proclaimed. Yet there is a profound link between this evangelization and human advancement. The person to be evangelized is not an abstraction but a human being living in very real economic, social, and political conditions. As Paul VI asked in 1975,

"How in fact can one proclaim the new commandment without promoting in justice and in peace the true, authentic advancement of man?" (Evangelization in the Modern World, 31).

It is an aspect of the church's mission of evangelization to stand with the poor. It is a duty of those of us in the church who are blessed with abundant gifts and resources to both share with those less well off and to make a preferential option for the poor. Quite recently the Catholic bishops reflected upon what the practice of solidarity means for Catholics in a society like the United States. As members of a universal church we must be willing to transcend national boundaries and live in solidarity with the human community throughout the world. This means more than supporting programs of international assistance to countries in need, necessary though this is.

Solidarity also means we do our best to critique programs and policies of this nation to appreciate their impact especially upon the poor in other nations. "We are also citizens of a powerful democracy with enormous influence beyond our borders. As Catholics and Americans we are uniquely called to global solidarity" (Called to Global Solidarity, 1). This necessarily means that we evaluate economic agreements that take the world further along the path of globalization. We judge such arrangements (NAFTA, CAFTA, WTO, IMF) not only by how they serve producers and consumers in the United States, but especially by how they benefit or fail to serve the needs of people in other nations who still yearn for a livelihood reflective of their dignity.

Discussion

1. How do you relate your role as a good citizen of the United States to your place within the world community?

2. What does it mean to say Jesus' command to "love your neighbor" has universal implications?

3. Do you agree with the claim in Catholic social teaching that no nation can remain prosperous for long if other nations are in serious poverty? Why, or why not?

4. In your own words explain the meaning of Pope John Paul II's statement: "Peace as the fruit of solidarity."

Actions

1. Invite an immigrant to speak in your parish about her decision to come to the United States. What challenges do people in her home country now experience? How might your parish respond to these challenges and needs?

2. Contact your diocesan mission office about developing a sister-parish relationship with a church in another country. What's involved? What might be the benefits of such a relationship? Is this something your parish can do?

3. Identify two ways you can promote the solidarity that leads to peace.

Chapter 8

Care for God's Creation

Rick and June finally decided to make the change. For many years they had run their farm like any other conventional dairy operation with high debts, low profits, and little time for anything but work on the farm. Most troubling to Rick was their increasing dependence upon chemical inputs for both crops and the dairy herd. He felt there had to be a safer way to produce milk—safer for the family and for the environment. They made the change and after several difficult transition years are now a certified organic dairy farm. That change has brought other benefits. Their children are more involved in the labor intensive aspects of rotational grazing for the dairy herd. Everyone enjoys the increased presence of wildlife on the now cleaner and healthier land and water. With more free time, Rick has made service and church mission trips to Haiti, Guatemala, and Mexico. The changes Rick and June made in their farming operation led to changes in their lifestyle—more attention to their family, to creation, and to people in other parts of the world.

ॐ

Caring for God's creation is a theme with relatively recent origins in Catholic social teachings. Over most of the past century these documents have little to say about humankind's relationship to the rest of creation. When the topic does surface, its focus usually lands upon some aspect of humans' superior status in relation to other creatures. It is not until 1990 that we have a papal document devoted entirely to caring for the environment. Pope John Paul II's World Day of Peace message, The Ecological Crisis: A Common Responsibility, presented new ways for Catholics to think about their responsibility for the earth. National bishops' conferences in different parts of the world soon followed with their own environmental statements. Among these is the United States Catholic bishops' pastoral statement, Renewing the Earth, a thorough summary of Catholic social teaching related to the environment. While this teaching on caring for creation draws freely from the Scriptures, it also relies upon the other core themes already discussed.

Creation is God's

The starting point for discussing humankind's place within creation is the simple recognition that all of creation belongs to God. Psalm 24 makes the point: "The earth is the Lord's and all that is in it, the world, and those who dwell in it" (v. 1). The first chapter of the first book of the Bible provides a creation story that may be debated from a modern scientific or historical perspective but is clear in its theological or religious intent. The writers are telling us something about their God who creates out of love and provides generously for those whom he has created. Never lost in this story is the message that their God is the one who creates, the one to whom everything belongs. Humans may be given a special place and responsibility among all the creatures, but their unique status is always in service to the Creator. The passing or temporary character of humans within creation is stated throughout the Scriptures, perhaps nowhere as bluntly as in the directives regarding the Sabbath laws in the book of Leviticus: "The land shall not be sold into perpetuity, for the land is mine; with me you are but strangers and guests" (25:23).

This biblical claim regarding God's ownership of creation and God's care in providing for all was an important factor in the decision of Rick and June to change their farming practices. That biblical claim also becomes the basis of the central themes in Catholic social teaching. The universal purpose of the goods of creation stems directly from this. Our responsibility to share with those in need is likewise rooted in this belief that whatever we have is a gift from God to satisfy our needs and those of our neighbor. The limitations on private ownership stem from this recognition that all belongs to God and all that we own or possess must be used with an eye to the needs of the larger community.

So also, our appreciation of humankind's place within creation must be connected to this recognition that everything is God's. Whatever else we may say about human rights and responsibilities on the earth or in the greater universe, nothing is more foundational than this acknowledgement that the earth is the Lord's and that we are but passing visitors. As guests we are obliged to treat with love and appreciation the surroundings we have been granted, and to use these gifts as the creator-owner intended. From the Scriptures, the early Christian writers, and from Catholic social teaching we can conclude that God intends for us to use his creation to meet our needs, to share it with our neighbors, and to preserve it for future members of God's family.

Creation is Good

Over the centuries Christian theologians and scientists have written extensively about humankind's place within creation. Much of that literature speaks of human's exalted role among God's creatures. Drawing from the first creation story, especially Genesis 1:26-28, writers often emphasized God's instruction to Adam and Eve to "increase and multiply" and to "subdue the earth and have dominion over" the rest of creation. Less attention was directed to an understanding of what the biblical sources intended to teach by the command to "have dominion over." There was little recognition that the term means primarily to watch over with love and care, to nurture, and to look after and protect—especially the vulnerable and the poor. This early literature likewise had little interest in showing how good creation is. As Catholic social teaching begins to address humankind's place and responsibility within creation, these topics begin to emerge. The goodness of creation, in particular, receives increasing attention in social documents addressing the environment.

And God saw

In the first creation story (Gen 1:1–2:3) the goodness of creation is affirmed at the outset. God ends each day by looking upon what he has created and declaring it to be good. "And God saw that it was good" follows God's creation of the earth, the oceans, the moon, the stars and sun, the vegetation, and the animals. All are created and deemed good even before humans enter the story of creation. Pope John Paul II acknowledges the goodness of creation without humans when he notes how often the Bible speaks about the goodness and beauty of creation "which is called to glorify God" (The Ecological Crisis, 14). Its magnificence is a source of wonder. Human contemplation of this aesthetic work brings peace and serenity (Ps 104).

John Paul II also reflects on how human sin has marred this wondrous creation. By acting against the Creator's plan humans destroyed the harmony within creation, alienating themselves from God, from one another, and even from the earth (Gen 3:17-19; 4:12). "All of creation became subject to futility, waiting in a mysterious way to be set free and to obtain a glorious liberty together with all the children of God [cf. Rom 8:20-21]" (The Ecological Crisis, 3).

The Holy Father further suggests that creation somehow will share in the redeeming work of Jesus Christ. He cites Ephesians (1:9-10) and Colossians (1:19-20) in stating that God will reconcile all things to himself through the death and resurrection of Christ—all things in heaven and all things on earth. The goodness, brokenness, and restoration of creation is the biblical message. That message informs Catholic social teaching, as is evident in this summary statement from John Paul II: "Creation was thus made new [cf. Rev 21:5]. Once subjected to the bondage of sin and decay [cf. Rom 8:21], it has now received new life while 'we wait for new heavens and a new earth in which righteousness dwells [2 Pet 3:13]'" (The Ecological Crisis, 4).

Sacramental universe

The goodness of creation is seen also in the fact that we humans are able to encounter God in a particular way through creation. God is present to us through nature. Our own environment is sacramental. It is through these created gifts of nature that we come into contact with the Creator. In their pastoral statement, Renewing the Earth, the U.S. Catholic bishops expand on this point:

> For the very plants and animals, mountains and oceans, which in their loveliness and sublimity lift our minds to God, by their fragility and perishing likewise cry out, "We have not made ourselves." (6)

Our Catholic worship places great emphasis upon the sacramental life. In ritual and in daily life we encounter God through the ordinary, material aspects of life. Our liturgical celebration of the sacraments relies upon the created goods of water, oil, bread, and wine to share in God's love and friendship. The bishops remind us how mystics of earlier centuries appreciated the presence of God in the very things God had made. The world in which we live is a "sacramental universe—a world that discloses the Creator's presence by visible and tangible signs" (Renewing the Earth, 6). Majestic mountains and canyons are places to appreciate the creative presence of God. So too are the farms, gardens, and lawns God has placed in our care.

The goodness we find in creation is a reflection of the goodness of the Creator. St. Thomas Aquinas taught that the reason the earth has such an incredible diversity of species is to more adequately reflect God's glory. No one creature—not even humans—could represent the divine beauty and goodness. For that reason God "produced many and diverse creatures, so that what was wanting to one in representation of the divine goodness might be supplied by another . . . " (ST, Prima Pars, q. 48, a.2). From that perspective, although it is right for humans to use the gifts of creation, it is also necessary that we show respect. Pollution of air or water is a failure to demonstrate that respect, and it is a barrier to encountering God in this sacramental world. A measure of humility and a willingness to sacrifice might help prevent our dishonoring the Creator by abusing the gift of creation.

Deserving of respect

Pope John Paul II offered a most practical reason for respecting this good creation: it is limited. All natural resources are limited in some way. For humans to use these gifts in the manner God intended, we need to respect this limitation. We also need to respect the connections and interdependence among all created beings, whether living or inanimate. Our own economic needs must not be the only consideration in determining how we use nature. Responsible interaction with creation reflects an awareness of the uniqueness of each being and of the interdependence of all (On Social Concern, 34).

The most basic reason for taking care of creation is found outside of ourselves and our own needs. Our faith calls us to care for what God has created simply because it is good and deserving of our respect. At the end of his message, "Peace with God the Creator, Peace with All of Creation," John Paul II expressed a desire "to address directly my brothers and sisters in the Catholic Church." He reminded us of our obligation to care for all creation and to commit ourselves to a healthy environment because of our belief in God the Creator. He then made one of the most powerful statements in Catholic social teaching regarding care for God's creation:

> Respect for life and for the dignity of the human person extends also to the rest of creation, which is called to join man in praising God [cf. Ps 96; 148]. (The Ecological Crisis, 16)

The dignity of the human person is the foundation of all Catholic social teaching. The right to life and respect for human life are central to Catholic piety. Pope John Paul II asks us to take one more step and recognize that respect for human life and respect for nature cannot be separated. In Renewing the Earth the bishops write that we should look upon nature and especially other species "not just as means to human fulfillment but also as God's creatures, possessing an independent value, worthy of our respect and care" (7).

All of creation gives glory to God its creator. Other species and the ecosystems themselves enjoy their own God-given purpose apart from whatever benefit they offer humans. The covenant God gave to Noah after the great flood was not just for humans; it was a promise to all the earth (Gen 9:9-17). Humankind's inability to appreciate the goodness of creation reflects an inability to appreciate the work of the Creator. It is a failure to see in the natural world the providing hand of a loving and sustaining God. Our mistreatment of the natural world is not only a failure to respect what God has created. It is also a failure to appreciate our own dignity and sacredness. For in abusing the earth we are endangering the life-supporting resources that we and future generations will need. Most importantly, we fail to carry out the task that God has assigned to humans: the care of creation. Thus, when we abuse the earth we engage in actions that contradict what it means to be human (Renewing the Earth, 2).

From a Catholic perspective, we need to find a balance between caring for humans and caring for the rest of God's creation. There should be no tension between the two and neither one contradicts the other. Centuries of teaching, however, have often granted an exaggerated status to humans within creation, as if we are above and not part of the created order. Our tradition's emphasis upon the dignity of the human person and the relatively late attention to caring for the earth have added to the challenge. Clearly one of our tasks is to see the relationship between this emphasis upon the life and dignity of humans on the one hand, and responsibility to care for all of God's creation (Renewing the Earth, 13) on the other. Rick and June's effort to take care of their environment and to help others in Guatemala is a search for that balance.

Humans and Creation

The creation stories in the opening pages of the Bible make it clear that humans have a special place within the natural world. The first chapter of Genesis speaks of humans being made in the image of God, and being told to exercise dominion over the rest of creation. In the second chapter we read that the man is placed in the garden to "cultivate and care for it." In each of these accounts humans alone are given the responsibility to look after what God has made. Biblical scholars contend that the command "to have dominion over" in Genesis 1 is best understood as exercising authority in the place of God and ruling as God rules—with compassion, love, and care especially for the vulnerable and the poor. The command in Genesis 2 to cultivate and care for the garden supports this emerging theme that humans share both a special place and a particular responsibility among all the creatures God has made.

Special place within creation

Catholic social teaching reflects this biblical sense of humankind's place of responsibility within creation. In his first encyclical letter, Redeemer of Man, Pope John Paul II warned against viewing the natural world in an exploitative manner. He noted that humans too often see their natural environment only in terms of how it might serve their immediate use and consumption (Redeemer of Man, 15). Earlier documents referred to humans' responsibility to care for the earth and to perfect it through intelligent labor (The Church in the Modern World, 57; On the Development of Peoples, 22).

The U.S. Catholic bishops summarize this thinking in Renewing the Earth: "Stewardship implies that we must both care for creation according to standards that are not of our own making and at the same time be resourceful in finding ways to make it flourish. It is a difficult balance, requiring both a sense of limits and a spirit of experimentation" (6).

Throughout the teachings there is this dual reading of our role and responsibility within creation. The first is to protect and care for the earth; the second is to enhance it, to make it flourish by our creative labor. John Paul II referred to this second task as cooperating with the Creator in the ongoing task of creating. The U.S. bishops term this responsibility as "God's stewards and co-creators" (Renewing the Earth, 12). Human stewardship of God's creation means respecting and caring for the earth because it is God's and because it is good. Stewardship also means working with creation so that it can satisfy human needs today and on into the future (Global Climate Change, 1). This includes making the fruits of our land available to others through the market mechanisms and through our support of trade agreements designed to benefit persons and countries who lack food.

Part of creation

As valid as it is to recognize humankind's special place within creation, it is equally important to recognize that we are part of creation. The second creation story in Genesis 2 makes this point with unmistakable clarity. Here there is no mention of humans being made in the image of God. Rather, the man is made "from the dust of the earth," from the same dust out of which God created the trees and the birds and the animals. All of us are made from the same stuff. All of us share a connection. Most significantly this story is a humbling reminder that we humans are more creatures than creators. We are part of the created order.

Our historical tendency is to see ourselves as more than citizens of God's creation. This is part of the meaning of Adam and Eve's choice to disobey God. It is both the cause and the consequence of our abuse of nature. John Paul II cautioned that such reckless exploitation of the earth not only threatens our natural environment, but also tends to remove us from nature. It allows us to see ourselves as separate from that which we do not respect (Redeemer of Man, 15).

Later, in The Ecological Crisis, the Holy Father wrote that we are so much a part of creation that our relationships and our activities impact nature itself:

> When man turns his back on the Creator's plan, he provokes a disorder which has inevitable repercussions on the rest of the created order. If man is not at peace with God, then the earth itself cannot be at peace [cf. Hos 4:3]. (5)

Renewing the Earth likewise reflects on this connection between our relationship with God and our care of creation. Awareness of the presence of God leads to experiencing ourselves as part of creation, not separate from it (6). That is one of the blessings of this sacramental world in which we live.

Sharers in God's gifts

Humans are to see themselves as members of God's created order, but members with a special role and unique responsibilities. The latter includes protecting nature and helping it to flourish. It also means striving to see that the gifts of creation—all the resources by which we live—are shared equitably among all God's people. Here a discussion of caring for creation necessarily draws from other themes in Catholic social teaching, notably the universal purpose of the goods of creation and the option for the poor and the vulnerable. Sharing the gift of creation is a basic Christian teaching from the earliest Christian writers to our own era. Misusing creation or hoarding land or water or other natural resources is a betrayal of God's purpose in creating these gifts for the sustenance and flourishing of all peoples.

Economic Justice for All summarizes the patristic teaching on this: "whatever belongs to God belongs to all" (34). All rights regarding ownership and use of property are subordinate to this more fundamental claim that God has provided sufficiently for humankind. It is our responsibility to see that these goods are shared on a reasonable basis, both within nations and among all countries. This common destination of earthly goods grants private property its social quality (The Church in the Modern World, 71). This principle also recommends the establishment between nations of trade relations that have particularly favorable terms for countries struggling to attain humane living conditions (On the Development of Peoples, 56–65).

Sharing God's earthly gifts so that everyone's needs are met is a significant way to respect this good earth and to honor our unique responsibilities as participants in creation. This obligation rests especially upon those persons and nations to whom God has been particularly generous. The earliest of Catholic social documents offered this simple, beautiful teaching.

> Whoever has received from the divine bounty a large share of blessings, whether they be external and corporal, or gifts of the mind, has received them for the purpose of using them for perfecting his own nature, and, at the same time, that he may employ them, as the minister of God's providence, for the benefit of others. (On the Condition of Labor, 19)

Though difficult to live out, the teaching is quite simple. Whatever we have, whatever we own legally, whatever we produce from the resources of nature—all of this is placed in our hands to be used for our own good and the good of others. It is with this in mind that the Second Vatican Council declared that all created things must be shared fairly by all humankind under the guidance of both justice and charity (The Church in the Modern World, 69). To do otherwise is an injustice, as John Paul II said in the first Catholic social document devoted to the environment:

> It is manifestly unjust that a privileged few should continue to accumulate excess goods, squandering available resources, while masses of people are living in conditions of misery at the very lowest level of subsistence. (The Ecological Crisis, 8)

This sharing of God's created gifts is a duty that extends over generations. We care for the earth and share its gifts among all peoples because of our respect for the Creator and this good creation. We protect the natural world also because of our responsibility to those who come after us. Not all natural resources are renewable; some are limited. To use these gifts in a way that endangers their availability to future generations is both an act against charity and a denial of our responsibility within creation.

Systemic change

Catholic social teaching reminds us as well that the poor and the powerless bear the greatest consequences from current environmental destruction. It is they who often live on lands that are most polluted, whose neighborhoods are designated for toxic waste storage, whose water is undrinkable (Renewing the Earth, 2). In many countries subsistence farming—itself the result of unjust land distribution—results in soil exhaustion and the steady destruction of forests to open new lands for survival farming. Because of this, Catholic teaching stresses that proper care of the environment cannot happen unless we address the structural forms of poverty (The Ecological Crisis, 11). Caring for the earth and caring for people go together, especially when the people are poor and vulnerable. They must be empowered to move out of poverty and to care for themselves in ways that do not destroy the natural environment. This means that the more affluent members of a society support changes in economic structures and public policies that make this possible.

It also means that more affluent nations engage in reform of trade agreements and other aspects of their relations with nations that suffer from high levels of poverty. Farmers in more developed nations, especially large, corporate style producers, have no legitimate claim to trade agreements that increase their income many times beyond their needs while producers in developing nations manage a subsistence living. The moral urgency of this imbalance is heightened when that subsistence farming involves practices harmful to the local environment. Rick's visits to such countries are not only about serving others. They also help him to see how our lifestyle in the United States is affecting people and the rest of creation in less developed areas. Care of creation today is not possible without a commitment to social justice and to the preferential option for the poor.

The church's concern for the dignity of work and the rights of workers also relates to care for God's creation. Workers and their rights must not pay the price for environmental protection. Too often protection of the environment is presented as a choice between jobs and a clean environment or between agriculture and preserving the natural habitat of a threatened species. Renewing the Earth firmly states that we must find solutions to environmental threats, but not in ways that "force us to choose between a decent environment and a decent life for workers" (8). It must never be a matter of choosing between workers and the environment. "Where jobs are lost, society must help in the process of economic conversion, so that not only the earth but also workers and their families are protected" (8). It is up to the broader community to provide support to workers in these situations. The burden of protecting the earth, the call to sacrifice in the face of new challenges to caring for creation, must not fall on workers or on those who are poor.

Lifestyles

Population growth is cited by many persons today as the greatest threat to the environment. With the current population well over six billion people and projected to continue increasing, many argue that these numbers go beyond the capacity of the earth. They also point out that the growing human population exacerbates every other environmental problem. More people create more pollution and make greater demands upon the earth's critical resources like soil and water. Catholic social teaching recognizes that the increasing human population presents challenges to caring for creation. In Renewing the Earth, the U.S. Catholic bishops state that "rapid population growth presents special problems and challenges that must be addressed in order to avoid damage done to the environment and to social development" (9).

This is not a call for curtailing world population growth, nor is it a plan for how these "special problems and challenges" should be addressed. Neither this document nor any previous social teachings in the church engage that discussion. What is significant about this statement is the fact that it is one of the first acknowledgements in the church's social teachings that the growth of the human population on this planet does in fact present a challenge to caring for creation. This recognition is even clearer when the bishops comment on the task of providing food for a growing population.

> Even though it is possible to feed a growing population, the ecological costs of doing so ought to be taken into account. (9)

Nonetheless, this teaching does not present population growth as the greatest threat to the environment. That threat comes from the lifestyle that is pursued in modern society. Pope John Paul II wrote that we will not solve the ecological problem unless we take a critical look at our lifestyles (The Ecological Crisis, 13). Earlier writings, such as Paul VI's A Call to Action, had sounded the alarm that humankind's careless exploitation of nature in support of an affluent lifestyle courts disaster. By so abusing nature we risk becoming the victims of our own actions (21). Likewise, the 1971 Synod of Bishops warned that the richer nations' demand for resources and energy, as well as their polluting the atmosphere and the oceans, posed a threat to all the world. They noted that if all humankind pursued such rates of consumption and pollution, "irreparable damage would be done to the essential elements of life on earth, such as air and water" (Justice in the World, 11).

These same concerns led the U.S. Catholic bishops to offer a critical evaluation of the impact Western lifestyles are having on the global environment.

> Consumption in developed nations remains the single greatest source of global environmental destruction. (Renewing the Earth, 9)

They note a growing awareness that this over-consumption by the industrialized world contributes more than any other cause to global environmental degradation. They also acknowledge that a child born in the United States is likely to place a greater burden on the world's natural resources than a child born in a developing country. For that reason and because of its abundant resources and world influence, the United States has a responsibility to offer leadership in caring for God's creation (Global Climate Change, 2).

There are many things we can do to protect the environment and correct patterns of past abuse. These actions range from individual recycling to employing less harmful technologies, especially in the area of energy use. They include enactment of laws and public policies that both encourage and mandate conservation and caring for the natural environment. Few of these efforts, however, will have the impact of our willingness as a people living in relative comfort to commit ourselves to a style of living less harmful to God's creation. That requires a sense of sacrifice and a sense of restraint. It requires that each of us considers our place and role within creation.

Not many of us are in a position to engage in organic farming, like Rick and June. We can, however, share their motivation to see our connectedness to the earth and to all people throughout the world. This requires that we daily live out the meaning of Christian love for our neighbor and for all of God's creation. It is not a matter of choosing to respect the neighbor or the earth. Renewing the Earth reminds us that our model is St. Francis of Assisi who preached to the birds and the animals only after a life of ministering to outcasts and lepers. We may not choose between people and the planet.

> At the heart of the Christian life lies the love of neighbor. The ecological crisis, as Pope John Paul II has urged, challenges us to extend our love to future generations and to the flourishing of all earth's creatures. But neither our duties to future generations nor our tending of the garden entrusted to our care ought to diminish our love for the present members of the human family, especially the poor and the disadvantaged. Both impoverished peoples and an imperiled planet demand our committed service. (Renewing the Earth, 11)

Discussion

1. Catholic social teaching emphasizes the biblical claim that all of creation belongs to God. This teaching also speaks of the universal purpose of the goods of creation. How does this fit with private ownership?

2. What does it mean to say that the world in which we live is a "sacramental universe"?

3. What does Pope John Paul II mean when he writes: "Respect for life and for the dignity of the human person extends also to the rest of creation"?

4. Reflect on Romans 8:20-21 and Ephesians 1:9-10. Are you comfortable with the thought that all of creation will share in some way in the redeeming work of Jesus Christ?

Actions

1. Identify one lifestyle change you can make to enhance awareness of your connectedness to the earth and to all people throughout the world.

2. Conduct an energy audit within the parish facilities and identify ways to reduce energy use.

3. Organize study and action groups around the bishops' pastoral statements: Global Climate Change and Renewing the Earth.

Epilogue

Meeting Lazarus

As disciples of Jesus Christ our challenge is to recognize and respond to Lazarus in our midst. That is one of the expectations flowing from our relationship with Christ. That is our path to hearing the Master proclaim:

> Come, you who are blessed by my Father. Inherit the kingdom prepared for you from the foundation of the world. For I was hungry and you gave me food, I was thirsty and you gave me drink, a stranger and you welcomed me, naked and you clothed me, ill and you cared for me, in prison and you visited me. (Matt 25:34-36)

The social teachings of the Catholic Church are a guide along this path, as are the many resources within the church that help us respond in love and justice to the Lazarus we meet in daily life. In his first encyclical, God is Love, Pope Benedict XVI reminds us that "love of neighbor is a path that leads to the encounter with God, and that closing our eyes to our neighbor also blinds us to God" (16). Our effort to respond to our neighbor, especially our neighbor in need—especially Lazarus—need not be a solitary effort. We are members of a church with people, programs, and materials to guide this response in charity and justice.

Living Catholic Social Teachings

Through baptism each of us is empowered to live our faith to the fullest and to participate in the ministry of the church. How we do this will depend upon the particular gifts God has given us and how we choose to use these gifts. Christian stewardship reminds us that God's gifts in us are given not solely for our own benefit, but must also serve the church in helping to build a more just and peaceful world. That too is a task of the entire church. Through its worship, catechesis, fellowship, and prophetic statements the Catholic Church witnesses to a transformed world. That witness shows forth at all levels of church structure.

Parish

All ministries within the parish should reflect this commitment to justice, to building a world that more closely reflects the reign of God that Jesus proclaimed. This is not a commitment that is limited to one parish committee or to a few individuals with a passion for social justice. Action on behalf of justice is a constituent dimension of the preaching of the gospel (Justice in the World, Introduction). As such it touches every aspect of parish ministry.

At the same time, there is a place and an important role for a social ministry committee in every parish. This committee may carry one of many names; its organization and functioning may differ from one parish to the next. Critical to the effectiveness of such a parish committee is clarity regarding purpose and goals. The Social Ministry Committee in St. Joseph's Church (ch. 5) has articulated three goals towards which all of its activities are directed: provide opportunities for parishioners to be involved in charity/service projects; provide opportunities for parishioners to be involved in justice/change projects; and, promote awareness of Catholic social teaching. The committee is the primary agent within the parish for leadership and resources regarding social justice. It serves as a liaison to all parish committees and ministries, helping each of them to bring into their work the gospel's call to justice. St. Joseph's Social Ministry Committee consciously strives to connect its work to the mission and core values of the parish.

Diocese

As in the parish, so also with the diocese there should be an intentional effort to incorporate the social justice implications of the gospel into every office and program. To that end a diocesan social concerns (or ministry, or justice) office can serve as a liaison and resource to all diocesan offices. An example of this could be a diocesan social concerns office

assisting Catholic schools as well as religious education and faith formation programs to incorporate Catholic social teachings into their
curricula.

The diocesan office can be helpful especially in supporting parish
efforts at social ministry, providing training and the necessary resources
for an effective parish program. This social concerns office is well posi-
tioned to help carry out educational programs in parishes around certain
annual collections—Catholic Campaign for Human Development, Catholic Relief Services, Migration and Refugee Services. The diocesan office
serves as a link between parish social ministry committees and national
and international justice programs.

State Catholic Conference

In most states the bishops have organized a state Catholic conference.
This is the public policy arm of the bishops within the state. Its task is
to identify, formulate, and seek to implement public policies that promote
the common good in accordance with Catholic social teachings. Typically
these conferences are organized around education and social justice
issues and their staff often includes a registered lobbyist.

The state Catholic conference can provide justice education and action
opportunities for parishes. The issues the conference addresses in the
state legislature signal to parishes what social justice concerns the bishops are addressing. Parish social ministry committees can work simultaneously on these issues through education and by organizing legislative
response networks that support the Catholic conference's work among
legislators. Connecting Catholic social teaching to current issues before
the state legislature—to issues in the daily news—can be an effective
way to engage parishioners with justice education.

United States Conference of Catholic Bishops

The United States Conference of Catholic Bishops (USCCB) is an
assembly of the Catholic bishops of this country working to unify, coordinate, promote, and carry out Catholic activities in the United States.
These activities include the ministries of justice and charity, and the
USCCB represents the Catholic Church in all matters of legislative and
public policy concerns at the nation's capital. Its pastoral letters are
timely responses to contemporary questions and challenges. Served by

a staff of more than 350 lay people, priests, deacons, and religious, the Conference is located in Washington, DC.

Within the USCCB are various offices and programs that have a particular bearing on diocesan and parish work for social justice. Among these is the Catholic Campaign for Human Development (CCHD), which seeks to transform lives and communities by focusing on breaking the cycle of poverty in thousands of local communities across the United States. It has a twofold mission of funding low-income, controlled empowerment projects and educating Catholics about the root causes of poverty. Most dioceses have their own (CCHD) office or person to serve as a liaison between the national program and parishes. CCHD's funding of empowerment projects, as well as its education program, offer great resources for dioceses and parishes to educate around the principles of Catholic social teaching.

Another example of a USCCB program that can be a helpful resource for the local church is the Office of Migration and Refugee Services (MRS), whose purpose is to serve and advocate for immigrants, refugees, and migrants. This office carries out its mission by helping to develop and advocate for public policy positions, by helping to resettle refugees, and by responding to the pastoral needs of persons within these populations. MRS can assist dioceses and parishes to sort out the many complicated matters surrounding this nation's current response to the immigration issue.

Yet another example of a national program to assist parish social ministry committees is the USCCB's Environmental Justice Program. This program calls Catholics to a deeper respect for God's creation and engages parishes in activities that deal with environmental problems, particularly those that affect the poor.

Within the USCCB, the entity most responsible for supporting diocesan and parish social justice actions is the Office of Domestic Social Development and World Peace, the national public policy agency of the United States Catholic bishops. This office seeks to promote greater awareness of the church's social teachings and to apply these teachings to major issues of the day. It advocates for the poor and the vulnerable and assists the church at all levels to act effectively in defending human life, dignity, and rights. This office and staff provide guidance and support to the various justice education and action programs of dioceses. It is the entity often responsible for assisting the bishops in drafting pastoral statements on current social issues.

Tapping the Resources

There are many programs and organizations whose activities and resources can benefit both individuals and parish efforts at social justice actions. Some of these operate within the formal structures of the Catholic Church, such as those discussed in the preceding pages. Others are Catholic in orientation and inspiration, but operate outside the structures of parish, diocese, or bishops' conferences. Still other helpful programs exist apart from the Catholic Church entirely and offer wonderful opportunities for engagement in social justice activity on an ecumenical or inter-faith basis. The following programs represent a few examples of the resources that are available to all of us.

Programs and offices within the local church

Parish Social Ministry Committee

> The name may vary from one parish to another.

Diocesan Social Concerns Office

> The name may vary. This program may be combined with the diocesan Catholic Campaign for Human Development, or it may be located within the diocesan Catholic Charities program.

Diocesan Mission Office

> Especially helpful in connecting parishes with the church in developing countries.

State Catholic Conference

National Catholic programs and offices

Social Development and World Peace
United States Conference of Catholic Bishops (USCCB)
3211 Fourth St., NE   (202) 541-3180
Washington, DC 20017   www.usccb.org

Catholic Campaign for Human Development
USCCB   (202) 251-3210
                                                      www.usccb.org/cchd/

Migration and Refugee Services   (202) 541-3352
USCCB   www.usccb.org/mrs/

Pro-Life Activities   (202) 541-3182
USCCB   www.usccb.org/prolife/

Environmental Justice Program   (202) 541-3182
USCCB   www.nccbuscc.org/sdwp/ejp/

Hispanic Affairs   (202) 541-3000
USCCB   www.usccb.org/hispanicaffairs/

Catholic Relief Services
209 W. Fayette St.   (410) 951-7280
Baltimore, MD 21201   www.crs.org

National Catholic Rural Life Office
4625 Beaver Ave.   (515) 270-2634
Des Moines, IA 50310   www.ncrlc.com

Additional faith-based justice and peace organizations

Amnesty International, USA
5 Penn Plaza — 14th Floor   (212) 807-8400
New York, NY 10001   www.amnestyusa.org

Bread for the World
50 F St. NW
Suite 500   (202) 639-9400
Washington, DC 20001   www.bread.org

The Catholic Worker
36 East First St.   (212) 777-9617
New York, NY 10003   www.catholicworker.org

National Council of Catholic Women
200 N Glebe Road
Suite 703   (703) 224-0990
Arlington, VA 22203   www.nccw.org

Network (A National Catholic Social Justice Lobby)
25 E Street NW
Suite 200   (202) 347-9797
Washington, DC 20001   www.networklobby.org

Oxfam International
1511 K St. NW   (202) 393-5333
Washington, DC 20005   www.oxfam.org

Pax Christi USA
532 W Eighth St.   (814) 453-4955
Erie, PA 16502   www.paxchristiusa.org

Reading the Documents

This book offers a brief look at the core themes and moral perspectives
that emerge from a reading of the Catholic social documents. These
themes offer guidance for living the social dimensions of the gospel and
they provide directions on how we might contribute to the building of
a more just and peaceful world. These themes are, however, only a starting point for engaging Catholic social teaching. For a deeper appreciation
of what our church has to say about justice and peace, nothing can sub-
stitute for reading the documents themselves.

Universal documents of Catholic social teaching

On the Condition of Labor *(Rerum Novarum)* 1891, Leo XIII

On Reconstructing the Social Order *(Quadragesimo Anno)* 1931, Pius XI

Christianity and Social Progress *(Mater et Magistra)* 1961, John XXIII

Peace on Earth *(Pacem in Terris)* 1963, John XXIII

Pastoral Constitution on the Church in the Modern World *(Gaudium et Spes)* 1965,
    Vatican Council II

On the Development of Peoples *(Populorum Progressio)* 1967, Paul VI

A Call to Action *(Octogesima Adveniens)* 1971, Paul VI

Justice in the World *(Justitia in Mundo)* 1971, Synod of Bishops

Evangelization in the Modern World *(Evangelii Nuntiandi)* 1975, Paul VI

On Human Work *(Laborem Exercens)* 1981, John Paul II

On Social Concern *(Sollicitudo Rei Socialis)* 1987, John Paul II

On the Hundredth Anniversary of *Rerum Novarum (Centesimus Annus)* 1991, John
    Paul II

Documents from the U.S. Catholic Bishops

The Challenge of Peace: God's Promise and Our Response, 1983

Economic Justice for All, 1986

Renewing the Earth: An Invitation to Reflection and Action on the Environment in Light of Catholic Social Teaching, 1991

Called to Global Solidarity: International Challenges for U.S. Parishes, 1997

Welcoming the Stranger Among Us: Unity and Diversity, 2000

Communities of Salt and Light: Reflections on the Social Mission of the Parish, 4th ed., 2001

Global Climate Change: A Plea for Dialogue, Prudence and the Common Good, 2001

A Place at the Table: A Catholic Recommitment to Overcome Poverty and to Respect the Dignity of All God's Creatures, 2002

Strangers No Longer: Together on the Journey of Hope (A Pastoral Letter Concerning Migration from the Catholic Bishops of Mexico and the United States, 2003

Faithful Citizenship: A Catholic Call to Political Responsibility, 2003

For I Was Hungry & You Gave Me Food: Catholic Reflections on Food, Farmers, and Farmworkers, 2004

Additional documents used in this book

The Ecological Crisis: A Common Responsibility (World Day of Peace Message) John Paul II, 1990

From the Justice of Each Comes Peace for All (World Day of Peace Message) John Paul II, 1998

Peace on Earth to Those Whom God Loves (World Day of Peace Message) John Paul II, 2000

God is Love *(Deus Caritas Est)* Benedict XVI, 2006